G000253072

'This book and study guide is a valu[..] conversation.'

— Andrew Nunn, Dean of Southwark

'The sexuality debate has become sterile in the church. Mandy Ford's *God, Gender, Sex and Marriage* provides an accessible, never over-simplified, account of the issues that bedevil the Church around gender and sexuality. Ideal for study groups, excellent as a discussion resource between progressives and conservatives, a model for "good conversation" where "bad disagreement" is too often what we settle for.'

— Canon Simon Butler, Prolocutor of Canterbury (General Synod)

'Drawing on social and church history, psychology and philosophy, on experience and Christian tradition, Mandy invites the reader into the complexity of gender, marriage, desire, sexuality and identity. Rather than provide answers, Mandy invites the reader to respond personally by offering thoughtful questions. This thoughtful book enables careful conversations with others with whom we might disagree.'

— Sandra Cobbin, trainer, coach and mediator, and facilitator for the Church of England Shared Conversation on Human Sexuality

'This book is a delight. It is lucid, elegant, learned, highly informative, compassionate, and totally free from rhetoric. It is a book written by a very gifted facilitator and a book that is itself a significant gift from her to her readers. She concludes her introduction with the words: "[this book is] the gift I want to share with you". I, for one, am very grateful.'

— Stephen Ruttle, QC and mediator, and facilitator for the Church of England Shared Conversation on Human Sexuality

God, Gender, Sex and Marriage

of related interest

God-Curious
Exploring Eternal Questions
Stephen Cherry
ISBN 978 1 78592 199 5
eISBN 978 1 78450 473 1

Forgiveness in Practice
Edited by Stephen Hance
ISBN 978 1 84905 552 9
eISBN 978 0 85700 983 8

Sceptical Christianity
Exploring Credible Belief
Robert Reiss
ISBN 978 1 78592 062 2
eISBN 978 1 78450 318 5

Can I tell you about Gender Diversity?
A guide for friends, family and professionals
CJ Atkinson
Illustrated by Olly Pike
ISBN 978 1 78592 105 6
eISBN 978 1 78450 367 3
Part of the *Can I tell you about...?* series

Doorkins the Cathedral Cat
Lisa Gutwein
Illustrated by Rowan Ambrose
ISBN 978 1 78592 357 9
eISBN 978 1 78450 696 4

GOD, GENDER, SEX AND MARRIAGE

Mandy Ford

Jessica Kingsley *Publishers*
London and Philadelphia

Scripture quotations are from New Revised Standard Version Bible: Anglicized Edition, copyright © 1989, 1995 National Council of the Churches of Christ in the United States of America. Used by permission. All rights reserved.

First published in 2019
by Jessica Kingsley Publishers
73 Collier Street
London N1 9BE, UK
and
400 Market Street, Suite 400
Philadelphia, PA 19106, USA

www.jkp.com

Copyright © Mandy Ford 2019

Front cover image source: Auguste Rodin, The Embrace (John Stewart Kennedy Fund, 1910).

All rights reserved. No part of this publication may be reproduced in any material form (including photocopying, storing in any medium by electronic means or transmitting) without the written permission of the copyright owner except in accordance with the provisions of the law or under terms of a licence issued in the UK by the Copyright Licensing Agency Ltd. www.cla.co.uk or in overseas territories by the relevant reproduction rights organisation, for details see www.ifrro.org. Applications for the copyright owner's written permission to reproduce any part of this publication should be addressed to the publisher.

Warning: The doing of an unauthorised act in relation to a copyright work may result in both a civil claim for damages and criminal prosecution.

Library of Congress Cataloging in Publication Data
Names: Ford, Mandy, author.
Title: God, gender, sex, and marriage / Mandy Ford.
Description: Philadelphia : Jessica Kingsley Publishers, 2018. | Includes
  bibliographical references.
Identifiers: LCCN 2018024738 | ISBN 9781785924750
Subjects: LCSH: Church of England--Doctrines. | Sex--Religious
  aspects--Church of England. | Marriage--Religious aspects--Church of
  England.
Classification: LCC BX5131.3 .F67 2018 | DDC 261.8/35088283--
dc23 LC record available at https://lccn.loc.gov/2018024738

British Library Cataloguing in Publication Data
A CIP catalogue record for this book is available from the British Library

ISBN 978 1 78592 475 0
eISBN 978 1 78450 860 9

Printed and bound in Great Britain

CONTENTS

INTRODUCTION

I'm assuming that you picked up this book because you are curious, and that is a great place to start! Perhaps you have a position about the topics covered and wonder how you might defend it. Perhaps you have discovered that others disagree with you, and wonder where their ideas are coming from.

This book came about because I observed people of good heart trying to explore ideas about gender, sex and marriage with each other and struggling to do so. Partly this is because these issues, which involve identity, personal behaviour and the good of society, are very complicated and partly it is because we have often arrived at our positions using different evidence, methods or even world views.

In researching and writing this book, I've been constantly reminded just what an amazing thing our relationships with other humans are and how through them we come to know and understand ourselves. It turns out that it is possible to use the questions about gender, sex and marriage as a way to go deeper into some of the most challenging questions that humans ask. Don't expect to find answers here, but do be prepared to encounter some very great mysteries, and to get some insight into the complexities of existence.

For those who believe in God, the mystery of existence is fundamentally tied up with the mystery of Creation and the Creator. As a Christian, I'm curious about the way in which humans relate to God and relate to each other as fellow creatures. In my experience there is a huge range of views of what it means to be human, loving and sexually active within the Christian church – at least as much diversity as there is between Christians and those with different religious allegiance or no faith at all.

Because many Christians (particularly Anglicans) will draw on science and philosophy as well as the Bible and church teaching to shape their views, you will find secular views discussed in this book alongside religious ones. For this reason, I hope that the book will provide a resource for anyone who is curious about human identity and behaviour to explore these questions.

Initially, I was reluctant to write this book because I was rather tired of talking about sex within a church context. As you will discover, gender and sex have been on the agenda of the Church of England since the 1930s. And surprisingly, despite the very small number of people who worship in the Church of England, Sunday by Sunday, there is still media interest in what the church believes and practises with regard to issues of gender, sex and marriage. Rowan Williams, the former Archbishop of Canterbury, has suggested that this is because the church provides a context where the moral anxieties and deep-seated questions that face society can be worked out. Perhaps there is a wider understanding that there is more to all this than just 'gay marriage' – that the church is asking the same questions about human identity, relationships and family that matter to all of us.

Even if you are not a person of faith, or a Christian, I hope that there will be questions in this book which interest you. And if you are a Christian, I hope that you will find the questions being asked relevant to you in your journey with God and with other people. We all have bodies and we all have desires. That means that we all have to make choices about how we use our bodies and how we meet, or control, our desires. That means that the topics covered in this book impact on each of us and are deeply personal. They affect real people with real lives and real relationships.

In the past five years it has been my privilege to help facilitate a series of 'Shared Conversations' between people in the Church of

England about 'human sexuality'.[1] This has been part of an organised process aimed at helping the church to listen better, prior to making decisions about its teaching and practice. That process has been hard. In those conversations people have shared their life stories and their faith stories. That has been personal and sometimes painful. They have also listened, often to those whose life experiences and faith are significantly different from their own. And that has been harder still. It is hard to listen to someone speak of their same-sex partner with love and affection when your whole heart and mind believes that same-sex activity is wrong. Some people have heard others tell them that their life choices put them beyond God's loving purpose for their lives. Many faithful Christians have been faced with the huge sadness of believing that friends and family members are condemned to a life without God because of the choices they have made.

As you read this book, you may find yourself reading things which you also find painful. I hope that will help you to appreciate that the same is true for people who may take a very different perspective to you. You will also discover that this is a very complex issue, in which it is not always easy to work out the truth or the right way forward. People have found conversations about gender, sex and marriage very painful because they have seen just how great the differences are between people of good faith, and have discovered how a way forward which seems life affirming and positive to one person may force another to leave the church which has nurtured them.

For some people, the fact that the 'Shared Conversations' in human sexuality took place at all reflected a wrong move on the part of the church. For those people, this book could also be cited as an example of 'false teaching' because it does not simply restate the existing teaching of the church. While I respect that view, it seems to me that the church has moved some way from a simple restatement that, for example, marriage between a man and a woman is the only acceptable context for a sexual relationship, and is now left with something which is neither coherent nor easy to communicate. If the church is going to restate its historic doctrines they will need to be proclaimed afresh to a new generation in a way that does not seem discriminatory but loving. While some Christians are able to do this in an attractive and life-affirming way, others are simply heard as being sexist or homophobic.

I am not trying here to suggest a solution to the church's dilemma or to offer a programme for change. My purpose is rather to resource people in continuing to reflect on the issues, and to offer some further questions. Other books have done this, in more detail and with more theological depth than is possible here, and I am grateful to them for providing much of the raw material for my own deliberations. However, to some extent they were books primarily intended for students of theology, or for clergy and decision makers. This book emerged, first, from some concern that many lay people in the church were ill-equipped to join the conversation that was taking place; second, from a request from the congregation at Southwark Cathedral, where I serve, for study material to inform their reflections; and finally, in the hope that others might want to be better informed about the Christian perspective on these issues.

All the conversations I have facilitated have taken place in Britain among people who live in a First World culture, which has a particular emphasis on individual choice, and in which family ties and commitments are fluid and economic survival is not a daily anxiety. From time to time, it has been good to remember that we are part of a wider church which includes many members across the world whose experience and priorities are significantly different. They have inherited a Christian tradition transmitted through colonisation and missionary endeavour, which is now being destabilised by changes in the culture from which it originated. There are some places where that destabilisation (which some think of as 'revisionism') threatens the mission of the church and its influence over the moral and ethical life of nations.

Before you jump to the conclusion that Christianity is holding back progress in the developing world, you might remember that it has also brought greater dignity and honour to women: it has been a means of challenging patriarchy (as well as upholding it), of questioning polygamy, and of honouring the marriage bond in societies where men have claimed the monopoly on choices about divorce. In some contexts it has been a force for good in curbing the abuse of children, particularly those forced into prostitution.

As you read this book, I hope that you will do so with a degree of openness to the experience of others – in particular those with whom you disagree. I have tried to write the book in that spirit and represent a spectrum of views as fairly as I can. I am sure that my own biases, conscious and unconscious, will be present, and I ask for your forgiveness when that makes the book difficult to read for you. I ought also to point out that this is a book written out of the Western philosophical and hermeneutical tradition – even the long words betray the problem! (By the way, hermeneutics is the study of interpretation, particularly the interpretation of signs and symbols, such as words and written language.) I'm particularly intrigued by the interface between what people believe, especially what they believe when they read the Bible, and how they behave. I'm interested in this topic as an intellectual dilemma and a social phenomenon. But I'm also aware that you won't find much personal story telling in this book. I hope that you will bring your own story, and the stories of people you know, to this book. And if you find something here that you don't recognise, that you might find someone to talk to who will tell their story through that lens.

I have made some decisions about the language I've used in the book. As this book is intended for a general readership and not for a particular Christian constituency, I have chosen to use the term LGBTQIA+ (lesbian, gay, bisexual, transgender, queer, intersex, asexual and others) to describe anyone who does not experience their gender or sexuality as normatively male or female, or normatively heterosexual. As we get into the book I will explain why even this is a problematic and contested area, but I didn't want my reader to be stumbling over unfamiliar terms which might interrupt the flow of the text. As I've surveyed the history of sexual behaviour, in particular, I've tried to avoid anachronism, but to use the labels which would have been familiar in that period of history.

When I write about the church, I generally mean the Church of England, as this is the church to which I belong and whose rules and norms I have to follow as an Anglican priest. I've tried to represent the doctrine of the Church of England accurately, and to show how diverse the church is in its practice and theology, as it is lived out in parishes, chaplaincies and cathedrals in Britain today. The church is held together by its structures, the General Synod and bishops, by its laws and by its worship, but expresses its diversity in the teaching you might hear in sermons, in the practical welcome afforded to individuals (for example some churches are willing to hold services of celebration following civil partnerships, while others are not), and in the debates in General Synod, its ruling body, about who can be ordained or married. One of the things you will notice is that there is, and has always been, some distance between the teaching of the church and the practice of its individual members. The church as an institution has a variety of ways of responding to this dilemma.

As society has changed, there are areas where the church has changed its view and has expressed this in a change in theology. One example would be contraception. Since the 1930s the Church of England no longer teaches that the only purpose of sexual intercourse is the procreation of children, but recognises that sex is also a means of building up faithful, permanent and loving relationships in which both members of the couple can grow in holiness. For this reason, the church does not condemn the use of contraception.

There are other situations where the theological position remains the same but pastoral practice is more flexible. One example would be divorce. In this case the church still teaches that marriage is the lifelong union of one man and one woman, but at the same time recognises that marriages can end, and that a second marriage may bring life and spiritual growth to a couple. Thus the Church of

England will permit its clergy to officiate at a marriage where one or both of the participants has been previously married and divorced.

Finally, we will see that there are situations where the stated theological position is clear, but pastoral practice varies widely. An example would be in the attitude to LGBTQIA+ people in active sexual relationships. For every individual parish church which maintains the traditional teaching that sexual activity should be confined to within the marriage of a man and a woman, there is another which welcomes LGBTQIA+ people and would want to bless permanent, faithful sexual relationships between them.

This can make it difficult for people both inside and outside the church to know 'what the church teaches' and for Christians to find the resources to inform their conscience when seeking to articulate their views, or even to make ethical life decisions.

We ought, in some ways, to be grateful that the church is struggling with what it calls so euphemistically 'issues in human sexuality' in our age. It is a sign that it takes seriously the interface between what Christians say we believe and the way we behave. By contrast, it could well be argued that for much of the church's history there has been very little correlation between the two. We only have to consider the abuse of celibacy by the Renaissance popes, or the institutional response to the treatment of women and children, or the scandal of child abuse, to recognise that what the church teaches and what individual church leaders and members of congregations do are often wildly divergent.

So the fact that the church feels that it can no longer say one thing about sex and marriage, while tolerating a wide range of behaviour which clearly diverts from its teaching, ought to give us hope. Only by being willing to be open to the reality around us, in the world and in the church, can we begin to discern what might be God's will for human flourishing, or to have anything convincing to contribute to the wider debate. In our age, these questions of gender and sexual identity have become the locus of conversations which reveal deeper divisions over our understanding of God's revelation in nature and Scripture, which are often mirrored in wider society by divisions between, for example, essentialist and constructionist views of gender.

This is all particularly painful for those whose personal lives and identities are put under the microscope. One reason why we continue to be having these discussions is that they are fed by our anxiety about identity in the 21st century, and in particular about the relationship between our identity as individuals and our place in the network of communities to which we also long to belong. In our consumerist society, it can appear as if all aspects of identity are a matter of choice, as simple as choosing whether to wear a skirt or trousers. But lived experience tells us something different. Whether it is a matter of our genes, our upbringing, our culture or our life history, the way we see ourselves and describe ourselves is a deeply ingrained and personal matter – not simply a matter of choice. For this reason, we need to be sensitive in the way that we judge others and address them in dialogue (even the imaginary dialogue which will be going on in your head as you read), and in caring for ourselves when the political or theological becomes personal.

For Christians, discipleship, that is, a life following Christ, has to be worked out in community, in order to discover what holiness looks like for today. Within a local church, the Church of England, the wider Anglican Church and the universal church (that is, all Christians) one of our challenges is to acknowledge that what looks like holiness to us may look like blasphemy, rebellion or sin to other Christians. Christians will also disagree about the extent to which what is right for Christians is right for everyone else. Some Christians feel that the moral values they uphold, like the faith they profess, should be set apart from wider society and culture. Others look for dialogue between people of good will across faith positions, and beyond.

The Church of England is in an unusual position, because it is not just a collection of congregations, but a national church with both a legal status and a national purpose. People who do not attend church to worship are still entitled to expect the church to provide a wedding or funeral service. Many of our national occasions, including royal weddings, remembrance and memorial services, and thanksgivings, take place in church. The presence of bishops in the House of Lords means that the church is involved in the making of laws which govern moral behaviour, and conversely, when the church wants to change its own laws (canons) it must do so through Parliament.

Perhaps the final piece in this complex jigsaw is the huge generational difference in the way that people approach issues around gender and sexuality in the developed world and I've seen this, in particular, as I've heard younger and older people come together to talk about issues of human sexuality in the church.

For people who grew up in the fifties and sixties, what was once illegal and hidden has become commonplace and open, yet the formal teaching of the church has not changed. For a younger generation, the teaching of the church seems completely out of line with their own experience, but they have little understanding of the enormous and rapid change that has taken place in society in the past fifty years. No wonder people find themselves confused, and often surprised by the views of others who belong to the same family, or the same faith or even the same denomination.

As you embark on reading this book I hope you will find things that surprise you, things that challenge you, and things that inspire you. As I have researched it, I have found all those things, and they are the gift I want to share with you.

1
GENDER, SEX AND MARRIAGE TODAY

If you talk to someone of a different generation to you, or someone who comes from a different religious faith, or a different culture, you may well find that you have a very different view or expectation of gender roles, sexuality and marriage.

My mother, who grew up in the 1950s, expected to give up work as soon as she married, at the age of 21, and to live a life with very different priorities to my father, who was the breadwinner and very definitely head of the family. She always found it amazing that my brothers, who grew up in the 1970s and married in their thirties, were willing to change nappies and were better cooks than their spouses. A generation further on, my nephews and nieces will not only expect to work on an equal basis with their partners or spouses, but will negotiate household roles and be able to marry a partner of the same sex should they wish.

You may recognise this picture, or your family situation may be very different, but you will certainly notice that there has been change in the wider culture. One distinct difference is in the gap between the traditional teaching of the church and the legal status of certain aspects of sex and family life. Another is the gap between what the church teaches as moral and normative, and what society believes and does. The past fifty years have been years of very rapid change and it is not perhaps surprising that many, particularly older people and those with responsibilities for leadership in government and the church, find the situation destabilising and unsettling.

The 1960s and 1970s are sometimes called the years of the 'Sexual Revolution' and there were certainly a number of significant cultural changes with regard to gender, sex and marriage. Such changes include the provision of contraception (made available to all through the National Health Service in 1968), the legalisation of abortion and the decriminalisation of homosexual acts, both in 1967, and the Divorce Reform Act in 1969.

Changes in the law did not necessarily reflect widespread social change. During the 1960s it was still common for men to be arrested for soliciting sex in public lavatories ('cottaging') while bars or clubs catering for gay men or lesbian women were necessarily discreet or even secret. Homosexual acts in private may have been legal, but the majority of the population would not have considered them morally acceptable.

The 1970s saw a series of liberation movements, as minority groups fought for the right to equality in the workplace and social sphere. In Britain, the Gay Liberation Front was established in 1970 and the first National Women's Liberation Movement conference took place in the same year. *Gay News* and the radical feminist publication *Spare Rib* were both launched in 1972, the year of the first Gay Pride march. It was also a period when conception became possible without sexual intercourse, as the first 'test tube baby' was born in 1978.

This was a period in which diverse youth cultures flourished, with various tribes reflecting their identity through choices of dress and music. Many of the fashion choices were androgynous: both men and women adopting the close shaved haircut, tight jeans and Doc Martins of the skinheads, the dyed hair, ripped or bondage gear and piercings of the punk movement or the colourful historical references, makeup, ribbons and ruffles of the New Romantics.

But there were also indications that wider society wanted to restore traditional values and perhaps a sense that liberation and the so-called 'permissive society' had gone too far. When gay men began to contract a previously unknown disease, subsequently identified as HIV/AIDs (human immunodeficiency virus leading to acquired immunodeficiency syndrome) and dying from it, there was a widespread sense that homosexual activity was the cause of the disease – in other words that the disease had a moral dimension. The use of terms such as 'gay plague' and an advertising campaign for safe sexual practice that raised the fear factor with the strapline 'Don't die of ignorance!' contributed to this emotional climate.

In 1987, the General Synod of the Church of England was asked in a private member's motion to reassert the church's traditional teaching about the nature of marriage, and did so with a large majority. In the following year, the Conservative government passed 'Clause 28' of a local government bill which made it illegal to teach the acceptance of homosexuality as a 'pretended family relationship'.

While gay men were stigmatised by HIV/AIDs, they also became more visible beyond the subculture. It became clear that men from all walks of life were suffering from the disease. The first gay characters appeared in soap operas (*Brookside* in 1984 and *EastEnders* in 1986), portrayed as ordinary people and not the camp caricatures of comedy or pantomime. In 1994 the age of consent for sex between men was lowered to 18, and in 2000 to 16 – the same as that for heterosexual consent.

Gender reassignment surgery has been available in Britain since the late 1960s, but it was not until 2004 that people were able to apply to change their legal gender on birth certificates and passports. The introduction of equal marriage made it possible for people to change gender and remain married, whereas until that date those seeking gender reassignment who were married were required to divorce first.

Civil partnerships, which allowed same-sex couples to enter a legal contract similar to marriage, were introduced in Britain in 2005, followed by equal marriage in 2013.

You will be able to think of examples of changes that you have observed in the past ten years, although it is harder to know what will seem significant from the perspective of history. There is some evidence of younger people, at least in the First World, rejecting traditional gender or sexuality labels and seeing themselves and their sexual activity as more gender fluid[1] and also more likely to identify as bisexual.[2]

You will also be able to think about events which would have been inconceivable ten years ago, such as the artist and writer Grayson Perry receiving his CBE as his alter-ego Claire; Prince Harry marrying a divorcee in church; a man with a beard dressed as a woman winning the Eurovision Song Contest; Susan Calman being supported by her wife as a contestant in *Strictly Come Dancing*.

In this rapidly changing world, we all make choices about how we live and what we think a good life might look like. In the next chapter, I will say more about how Christians make those decisions and the kind of things that decision making draws upon. Some of them will be common to people of other faiths, and some will be common to people of no faith at all. All of us will be aware of the impact of our choices on ourselves, our family and friends, and perhaps on wider society.

Some Christians believe that their primary responsibility to others, including people in wider society, is to bring them to faith in Christ, since without such faith they are condemned to eternal separation from God. This is a serious claim with significant existential consequences made in love and obedience to a sincerely held understanding of God's purpose for humanity. In this view the church should be set apart, to be holy and pure, from a culture which has strayed far from Christian moral teaching. Many Christians who hold this view are able to do so with compassion and sympathy for people whose self-understanding or self-identification is LGBTQIA+, or who experience themselves as same-sex attracted.

The challenge for those who hold this traditional view of Christian moral teaching on gender, sex and marriage is to be heard by a society in which many people believe that the church is still sexist and homophobic. There are pastoral consequences, particularly for young people as they try to make sense of these issues, but for all LGBTQIA+ people who experience the church as discriminatory or oppressive. There is also a particular challenge in sharing the gospel with a younger generation who find traditional teaching hard to comprehend, as society's values – particularly those around equality, self-determination and freedom – seem to be so much in conflict with Christian moral values.

For others, the first priority of Jesus' commandment to love our neighbour is to meet people where they are and to discern what might be virtuous in their life choices. For Christians who want to acknowledge and accept LGBTQIA+ people on equal terms within a moral framework which includes marriage, they have to do so in the knowledge that they are moving significantly away from hundreds of years of Christian practice, tradition and theological understanding.

It is possible that the words used in this book will soon seem outdated and rather quaint, since they are so culturally determined. As you will see as you read on, there has been a great change in the way in which certain practices are now understood as markers of identity, and I have a sense that this will not necessarily last. It is possible that we are entering a paradigm shift, in which our understanding of human identity and human sexuality are becoming unrecognisable from traditional understandings. We will not know whether this is the case for many years and this is why the shift is so uncomfortable.

Questions

- What changes have you observed in people's attitudes, behaviour and in the law around gender, sex and marriage in your lifetime?
- How should the nation state or the church respond to those changes?

2
MAKING DECISIONS

All of us, whether we are people of faith or not, have to make ethical decisions in life. We make decisions about how we spend our money, the food we eat, the way we treat our friends and neighbours, and the way we shape our closest personal relationships.

In making those decisions we will be influenced by some things we are aware of, such as the values we were taught by our parents and the expectations of our culture, and some things that are more subconscious, such as the influence of advertising and social media.

It is often only when we find ourselves in conflict with others that we become aware of the decisions we have made, or the viewpoints we hold, and one of the challenges of contemporary life is the extent to which our experience has created unconscious bias towards people who already think like us. Take a moment to consider where you get your ideas about the world from: the websites you visit, the people you follow on social media, the programmes you watch. I'm guessing that in most cases, you get your ideas from people who are quite like you – in age, gender, language, culture and so on.

Of course, this is a generalisation and many of us are lucky enough to study or work in places where there are people who are not so much like us and don't think the same way that we do. I wonder about the quality of the conversations that you have and how you explore the differences in your ideas?

Conversations across difference are often very challenging. We are easily pushed back into simplistic positions and may seek to find others to support our viewpoint. This leads to the kind of factionalism that we see in so much of public life today. It also masks the deeper underlying paradigms (or belief systems) which shape people's views. For example, a meat eater and a vegetarian may disagree about their diets, but have both chosen their stance because they are interested in the survival of the planet. The meat eater believes that compassionately raised animals feeding on upland grass contribute to the ecosystem, while the vegetarian believes that it is better not to eat meat at all because so many farm animals are fed grain or soya which would be a valuable source of nutrition for humans, especially in poorer countries. Their underlying shared belief in the importance of the earth as a resource is masked by their disagreement about what to eat.

When discussing differing viewpoints, one of the questions we might ask is 'How do you know?' This may lead to us asking about evidence and the accuracy or truthfulness of that evidence. Of course, you can't challenge someone's own feelings about their lived experience. But you might ask how generally shared that experience is among other people and so how widely it can be applied. You might ask yourself whether the experience is backed up by knowledge and what kind of knowledge would be relevant. In the past, certain authorities would be widely trusted to provide well-informed and accurate evidence, but that has become degraded in recent years. There has been a lot of discussion about the so-called 'death of the expert' which suggests that people are not really interested in factual knowledge, or don't trust people who have acquired knowledge, but that is not quite the full picture. A survey by IpsosMORI in 2016 showed that people still trust doctors, scientists and teachers more than 'the man or woman in the street', but they don't trust journalists or politicians (and their trust in journalists and politicians, which was never high, has gone down in recent years).[1] However, if you then ask yourself where people get their information, you might not be surprised to know that about a third of young people get their news from social media – in other words it is passed on to them by other 'men and women in the street'.[2] If your news comes to you from your friends, or people like you, then you are likely to conclude that everyone thinks the same things that you do, or agrees with your point of view. There is evidence that many British people who wanted to remain in the European Union were surprised by the Brexit vote because they only saw news reports from other pro-remainers.[3]

So, there is a challenge for us when making decisions in knowing what sources of information to draw on and how trustworthy they are, and there is a further challenge in being able to look below the surface and see what underlying beliefs might inform our choices. Finally, we might want to think about what the decision making process looks like, particularly when it can't be reduced to a simple factual binary choice, either meat or no meat, for example.

How Christians make decisions

Anglicans make decisions on the basis of a balanced tension between three (or four) sources of authority: Scripture, tradition, reason (and bishops). This methodology has been worked out over time as an expression of the *via media*, or middle way, between Protestant and Catholic expressions of Christianity. With Protestants, the church recognises the individual's right to conscience and reading the Biblical texts for himself or herself, following Luther's premise that all that is needed for salvation can be found in the Bible. With Catholics, the church holds that the task of the church has always been to interpret what has been handed down and that this is the mechanism whereby understanding may be consolidated (tradition) or changed in the light of experience (reason). Anglicans also enjoy the heritage of theology embedded in their liturgy, and in the writings of their own poets, preachers and teachers. Appeals to reason, in which the application of scientific knowledge, social experience and other factors are brought to bear, are made on the assumption that God is at work in the whole of the world and is revealed in Creation. However, reason itself reminds us that we are fallible, as we observe how human understanding of nature changes, and that fallibility ought to lead to a certain reticence about any truth claims we make.

SCRIPTURE

Anglicans affirm the authority of Scripture as the way in which God communicates by his Spirit though the church. They will speak of Scripture as 'uniquely inspired witness to divine revelation' and 'the primary norm for Christian life and faith'.[4] The Bible is read and interpreted in church every Sunday and many Christians read the Bible as part of their private prayer and devotional life.

Let's think about what the Bible is, and then about what we are doing when we read the Bible. The Bible is a collection of writings dating from the eighth century BCE to the first century CE. Jesus and his followers would have known the Jewish Scriptures, the books we commonly refer to as the Old Testament. In turn, their story is told in the books and letters of the New Testament collected over two or three hundred years. Both were gathered together and gradually an agreed and authoritative canon became accepted across the Christian church in the third century CE. The process of agreeing which texts would be included was partly a process by which the church decided what it believed about Jesus. Texts which offered a view of Jesus that differed from the orthodox view were discarded. So, we are talking about a library which was built up over nine hundred years and contains texts of different styles or genres including history, law, poetry and prophesy.

While Christians agree that the Bible is the Word of God, they do not understand this in the same way that, for example, Muslims believe that the Q'ran is the directly breathed or dictated word of God. Rather, the Bible is the story of the relationship of the people of God with God, which demonstrates their unfolding understanding of God's purpose for Creation. The stories and teaching of Jesus represent a radical restating of God's purpose and its extension to people beyond the Jewish tribes of the Middle East. The whole Bible contains narrative history and poetry as well as teaching and the law. The law itself is expressed in a variety of forms, including the Ten Commandments in the Old Testament, and the 'Great Commandment' (Love God and love your neighbour as yourself), in the teaching of Jesus.

This means that when we read the Bible we ought to be sensitive to the genre of the text we are reading and to its context. Jesus himself interpreted the Scriptures that he knew, in the light of his own experience and purpose. He taught not only by using Scripture, but also by telling stories and through the example of his actions. In his actions, Jesus was ambivalent about the Jewish law embodied in the Scripture, as it was practised in his own time, in particular when it seemed to oppress the poor. In other words he both drew on Scripture and challenged it, both in his teaching and in his actions.

Making sense of the Bible might involve us in a few different ways of exploring the text. The first is to read it at face value, taking into account the genre or style of the section we are reading. We are not expected to read the text as if it was a puzzle to be solved or is deliberately hiding some secret or mystery from us. But we will probably approach poetry differently from law or narrative, just as today we don't read a novel expecting to find instructions for driving a car, or the Highway Code as a guide to relationships. Second, we also need to consider the historical setting of the text, its original authors and readers, and the sense that they would make of it. This might depend on their situation or setting, the original meaning of the language, and the cultural setting of the writer. It might mean paying particular attention to the meaning of a word, bearing in mind that, unless we are reading in Greek or Hebrew, we are reading a translation. Finally, we will want to place the text in the big picture – the overarching story of God's purpose for his people. We cannot 'extract' truth from the Bible, neither should we take a text out of its context, especially to prove a point (this practice is called 'proof texting').

Since the 19th century, there has been significant scholarship focused on unpacking the origins of the Bible and the social influences on its composition which recognise the very human cultural assumptions inherent in its world view. This scholarship has helped Christians to distinguish between the cultural norms of the first century CE, such as patriarchy or slavery, and deeper truths such as God's love for the whole of humanity.

These insights have helped Christians to recognise how their own cultural biases have shaped their reading of the Bible. For many years the church in South Africa was able to find justification for apartheid in the Bible. As theologians listened to the differing interpretation and experience of black readers of the Bible, this cultural racism was challenged. This helps to remind us of the important question, 'Who interprets?' Do we just assume that interpretation is always impossibly relativist and culturally determined, or do we try to enter into dialogue with Christians who see the world differently from us in order to seek common ground?

One thing seems clear: Christians cannot simply ignore the Bible, nor treat it as a text which can be interpreted to mean anything you like. Rather, we need to take it seriously, and to allow it to challenge us. This is what the Christians who abolished the slave trade did, allowing the Bible to challenge them to see all humans as created in God's image and so deserving equal rights and liberties. This is what individual Christians do, as they try to live as if the claims of the Bible are true.

As we will see, biblical texts often have to be brought into dialogue with one another in order to decide on moral or ethical priorities.

TRADITION

The Christian appeal to tradition is an appeal to the collected and historic wisdom of the church through the centuries. The value of this appeal lies in its awareness of the expanse of human history and the belief that there is some continuity in God's plan for Creation, but that it can evolve. The pace of change in the church is slow, but this helps to ensure consistency and continuity, not only in the church's teaching but also in its membership.

When we talk about 'tradition' we actually mean two things: the tradition handed down in an unchanging way through the history of the church, and the traditions of the church expressed, for example, in its worship. Some ideas which are central to Christian faith are not easily found expressed in the Bible. A good example of this would be the doctrine of the Trinity. Although there are texts which refer to God as Father, Son and Holy Spirit, the relationship between them as co-existent, co-equal and co-eternal had to be worked out through dialogue and councils over three centuries before it was fixed in the Nicene Creed in 381 CE.

The Nicene Creed is a good example of the way in which tradition is the product of history, shaped by power dynamics, politics and war as much as by wisdom, learning and cooperation. The Creed marks the triumph of one set of churches over another, yet that victory did not prevent the separation of the Eastern and Western Churches within a century or two.

The Church of England looks back in the tradition to the writings of the 'Fathers of the Church' in the early centuries and you will see Irenaeus (120–202), Augustine of Hippo (354–430), Clement of Alexandria (c. 150–c. 215), Gregory of Nyssa (c. 335–c. 395) quoted as authorities, as well as Anselm of Canterbury (1033–1109) and Thomas Aquinas (1225–1274). However, when reading these authorities, we have to bear in mind their very different philosophical and scientific understandings. From time to time, paradigm shifts in understanding have led to the church changing its view. A good example would be our understanding of the place of the earth in the solar system: we no longer believe in an unmoving planet around which the sun, stars and moon revolve (Psalm 93:1) since Galileo showed that the earth circles the sun.

The Church of England sees itself as both derived from an unbroken inheritance with the Roman Catholic Church and reformed, despite its break with Rome in the 16th century. There were many ups and downs before a final settlement in 1689, which has remained the basis of the constitutional position of the Church of England ever since, in which the church remains the established church with a range of particular legal privileges and responsibilities, but with ever-increasing religious and civil rights being granted to members of other Christian denominations, those of other faiths, and those professing no faith at all.

The Church of England became defined not only by its constitutional position but also by the adoption of a single form of worship, the 1664 Book of Common Prayer. The Book of Common Prayer defines what the church believes by prescribing the words used in worship. As we will see, this becomes particularly important when we consider what the church believes about marriage, which is mainly expressed not in teaching but in the marriage service.

Traditions can change and that can be seen in our worship too. The church is called upon to proclaim the gospel afresh in every age. It does this partly by changing the language it uses in worship so that it can be better understood. A good example is the way in which we now describe the third person of the Trinity. In the Book of Common Prayer you will find lots of references to the Holy Ghost. In the 16th century everyone understood that this was a spiritual person or entity. However, in the 21st century, we tend to think of ghosts in comic terms, as headless horsemen or spectres draped like white sheets. For this reason, the church now consistently uses the term 'Holy Spirit' instead of Holy Ghost. The church also reflects its changing understanding by providing new forms of worship, such as a service of blessing following a civil marriage.

REASON

The final appeal, the appeal to reason, is based on the assumption that if humans are created in the image of God, then God has given us intellects in order that we might more fully know God's purpose for us and for Creation.

Reason depends on rational thought, but it is important to recognise that this is limited by the understanding available to the culture at any point in history. The Church Fathers of the fourth century relied on Platonism; in the 13th century Aquinas drew on the philosophy of Aristotle; during the 18th-century Enlightenment, many theologians drew on Kant and you will find contemporary theologians who have been influenced by linguistic theory, by Heidegger, Derrida and Lyotard. Countering this engagement with rational philosophy, many theologians writing from outside Western culture have criticised the use of European philosophical categories, pointing to the importance of community discernment and dialogue as a means of discernment in African culture, for example.

The relationship between faith and reason is not straightforward and there have been times when the church has held on to its beliefs and refused to acknowledge the truth of science for a long time. The Roman Catholic Church was very slow to accept the scientific findings of Galileo, for example,[5] and early responses to Darwin's theory of evolution were equally dismissive. However, most modern interpreters of the Book of Genesis would not attempt to use the Bible as a reliable guide to our origins in any scientific sense.

Reason is sometimes equated with the idea of 'natural law', that is, the belief that we can see God's purpose in nature. In the early modern period, the exploration of the natural world was driven by the desire to know God through the 'book of the world', and the assumption that the underlying laws of nature and of physics were evidence of God's orderly plan for Creation.

Humans are curious about the world around us, both in a playful and creative way, and because we want to influence and master the world. Understanding the laws of physics and the natural world has enabled humans to do many good things: to alleviate suffering, to cure disease, to explore and appreciate the wonders of creation. For the past thousand years in the West, it has been assumed that we were intended to explore and uncover the 'laws' which governed the universe, for the benefit of all.

However, there is a danger that we then claim that what is 'natural' is what is intended to be, but this opens up all sorts of problems with regard to human behaviour such as aggression and selfishness. Equally, appeals to what is 'natural' or 'reasonable' are very vulnerable to changes in understanding and do not always travel well across cultural difference.

PUTTING IT ALL TOGETHER: MORALITY AND ETHICS

This is not the place for a long diversion into the complexities of morality and ethics. But I do want to highlight a couple of areas that you might want to bear in mind as you continue to read this book.

The first is that there is an assumption that religions will teach their adherents how to *behave* as well as what they should *believe*. This is particularly clear in Judaism and in the influence of Old Testament ethics (for example the Ten Commandments) on Christians, and thus on the moral life of much of Europe for many centuries.

However, the relationship between Old Testament law codes and 'right behaviour' for Christians has been problematic right from the beginning. Jesus' attitude to the Jewish law was ambivalent, at best. For Christians, the moral law begins with the Great Commandment (Matthew 22:35–40; Mark 12:28–34), 'You shall love the Lord your God with all your heart, and with all your soul, and with all your mind... You shall love your neighbour as yourself' (Matthew 22:37–39;

Mark 12:28–34). But whether this needed to be worked out by following not just the teaching of the Ten Commandments but also all the norms of Jewish law, including its dietary rules for example, became a problem as non-Jews began to follow the way of Jesus.

We can see in the letters of Paul and the Acts of the Apostles that the early church faced a significant challenge in working out the relationship between Jewish law and Christian moral living. Paul's letters grapple with specific problems which arose in new church communities, and in them we see a great deal of pragmatic realism alongside a strong critique of some pagan practices, particularly those connected with temple worship.

Second, even if we just take the core commandments, ethical problems can arise. Take the commandment about lying, 'You shall not bear false witness against your neighbour' (Exodus 20:16). So what do you do when an assassin knocks on the door with a knife in hand and asks if your brother is at home? Do you tell the truth, or do you lie to protect the innocent? This is a very simple example which serves to demonstrate that all moral laws exist in hierarchies and that the relationship between them may not always be clear.

So we need a way to sift ethical teaching. One way, which can be helpful, is to make a distinction between duties – that is the things we ought to do or ought not to do – and virtues – the things we might aspire to.

In European culture, the idea of duty is very closely tied to the philosophy of Immanuel Kant (1724–1804). Kant's idea of morality was that duties derived from universal truths so that choices about behaviour should be governed by a universal principle which applies in every situation. The duty to behave towards others as we would wish them to behave towards us fulfils this philosophical test, as does the duty not to harm others. The second duty, which Kant proposed, was that all humans should be treated as an end in themselves and not as objects or as the means to another end. You might notice that this philosophical description of moral behaviour is very close to the teaching of Jesus about loving your neighbour as yourself, and similar ideas are found in many world religions.

In philosophical terms, duties are tied to rights. They are part of the social contract whereby communities, both local and global, are enabled to live in an ordered way. They also challenge individuals and communities to consider the impact of their behaviour more widely, not simply on those with whom they have face-to-face contact, but with others who feel the impacts of their behaviour. This is a huge issue in a global world where we depend on people far away, who we will never meet, for our food and clothes. How often do you think about the person who has made the cheap T-shirt you are wearing, or who grew the tomatoes for your pizza sauce? But our consumption of clothes and food may lead to exploitation, or a job and a better standard of living, for workers in countries on the other side of the world. The rights of human beings were codified by the United Nations in the Universal Declaration of Human Rights adopted in 1948, but it is notable that a declaration of Human Duties and Responsibilities had to wait until 1998 and is a far less well-known document. It repeats Kant's duty to refrain from doing to others what you would not wish done to yourself, as well as the duty to treat every human being as an end, and not as a means or object.

Kant's ideas have been criticised because they assume that humans are to make informed decisions on the basis of these universal ideas, and to act in accordance with those decisions even when they are unpleasant or difficult for us. In particular, Kant makes no concession to the idea of desire, which he sees as a hindrance to the will. It is true that an appeal to duty can discipline desire when desire is selfish or self-serving, but desire itself can motivate us towards good ends. We might desire to be more unselfish, more thoughtful or more ethically aware.

This leads us to an alternative ethical model, that of 'virtue ethics'. The idea of virtues has its origins in the teachings of Plato

(427–347 BCE) developed by his student Aristotle (384–322 BCE), codifying the qualities that would lead to a person leading a happy life. Happiness does not simply refer to wellbeing, but to a deeper satisfaction with life lived well – so it has an ethical dimension. The four virtues on which all others hang were listed as prudence (or practical wisdom), temperance (or moderation), courage and justice. You might notice that none of these characteristics tell us exactly what kind of actions are required, instead they are descriptions which can be applied to actions.

Aristotle had a great influence on Christian moral teaching and in the sixth century theologians identified specifically Christian virtues: chastity, temperance, charity, diligence, patience, kindness and humility. Christians made a distinction between virtues which humans could strive for, and those which are gifts from God. The latter are the three virtues of faith, hope and love.

One of the advantages of virtue ethics is that it begins with a goal towards which we are working, rather than a stated and fixed position. It provides more space for individuals to make up their own minds. Its disadvantage is that it does not provide moral norms or standards of behaviour to be applied or tested in any situation. Virtue ethics can look very context specific, or situational, and thus is in danger of leading to a kind of moral relativism in which what is OK for me is not OK for you. For this reason, explorations of virtue ethics often lead us back to something that looks more like moral duty.

Take the example of secular marriage law. This was based on the idea that permanent, faithful, stable relationships were virtuous, something to be desired, leading to a good life. Marriage was seen as a good thing, but was not available to all couples because same-sex relationships were considered morally wrong. LGBTQIA+ people argued that they could also strive for virtuous partnerships, which should be protected by, and given the benefits of, legal status. The change in the law demonstrated a change in moral norms. Generally, for a society or a community to live together peacefully, we need such moral norms and they are expressed in our law. Other examples would be laws which forbid sexual activity with children, or which protect the equal treatment of men and women in the workplace. In this way society sets boundaries which protect the weak and defend equality. Agreeing moral norms is a challenging task for churches or nations, because the process requires people to discern what is good for the whole community and not just for some of its members or for the people in power.

You will find both approaches to ethics – the requirement to be obedient to duty and the desire to achieve virtue – in Christian teaching. You may find it helpful to hold the tension between the two in mind as you explore the issues in this book.

Of course, we all want to behave well and recognise that for various reasons we don't always do so. Christians explain this failure as 'sin', but there are other non-theological explanations, which may or may not have moral dimensions. The problem of the will (that is, our capacity to do what we think is right) preoccupied Kant and the philosophers of the Enlightenment. They were convinced that people could make moral choices on the basis of intellectual decisions. Part of the problem, which we now associate with the philosopher Descartes, was their tendency to separate out, and privilege, the intellect over the emotions and so to downplay aspects of desire that we can't easily control.

The forces that might shape our desires were explored in the early 19th century by three significant thinkers (sometimes called 'Masters of Suspicion'): Marx, Darwin and Freud. Each suggested that we are at the mercy of forces beyond our control, namely history, our biological drives and our subconscious urges. Marx reminds us of the part that political, social and financial power play in constraining or controlling the choices we can make in life, or the identities we can inhabit. This has been, and remains, particularly true for women. Darwin demonstrated that we are, like all animals, driven by the need for survival which influences our behaviour with regard to sex, food and power. Freud demonstrated how our early experience shapes our behaviour as adults. Although his model of the human psyche is not universally accepted, we now know much more about the way in which early experience can influence behaviour, including things like our propensity to take risks, act aggressively or seek pleasure. By becoming more aware of these forces at work in shaping desire we can make more informed choices, and perhaps recognise that mastery of the self is a challenging task!

We will be looking more closely at these challenges later in the book, in particular in Chapter 4, 'Desire'. But, as you can see, there are a lot of different factors at play when we are making decisions about our behaviour and trying to stick to the choices we think are best.

Before we go any further, I want to consider one other question about how we make decisions: what do we mean by conscience?

CONSCIENCE

The ancient Greeks considered that there was an organ of discernment by which individuals made moral choices and called this organ the conscience. Plato described its working as like hearing an inner voice or seeing an inner light. This description is more metaphorical than actual, as there is no identifiable organ of decision making, although we now know that decision making is linked to particular areas of the brain associated with our capacity to defer pleasure or to act in more measured or self-aware ways.

Early philosophers, such as Seneca and Cicero, thought that the conscience could be educated, but also that some people had inherent wisdom or aptitude for making good judgements.

Others have noticed that the idea of conscience is closely tied to the emotional experience of guilt or shame. Feeling guilt about one's behaviour is dependent on having a personal sense of morality and of right and wrong. Feeling shame may be driven either by the same internal personal sense, or by experiencing embarrassment for transgressing social norms. Developmental psychologists, in particular Piaget and Kohlberg, describe how conscience develops in childhood as the individual gains the capacity to take responsibility for their own actions and so knows when they have done wrong.

However, there is some dispute about whether conscience enables us to make choices ahead of our actions or is the way in which we assess and justify, or regret, our behaviour after the event.

Some contemporary philosophers have pointed out that there is also a social dimension to conscience. If you are starving, or your life is constantly threatened in a war zone, for example, you are less likely to be concerned, or to feel guilty, about stealing food or even killing another person. On the other hand, many people in the developed world seem remarkably free of any sense of guilt about the impact of their lifestyles and consumer choices on the people who make the goods they enjoy or the consumption of non-renewable resources.

Theologians, beginning with St Paul, recognise the idea of conscience but rather than explaining it purely in terms of personal choice, connect conscience to the divine moral law. St Paul considers that conscience demonstrates that anyone can know God's purpose, so that there is a relationship between natural law and conscience; writing in Romans (2:14–15):

> *When Gentiles, who do not possess the law, do instinctively what the law requires, these, though not having the law, are a law to themselves. They show that what the law requires is written on their hearts, to which their own conscience also bears witness.*

Here, conscience seems to act as a witness to the truth. Elsewhere (Corinthians 8:7, 10, 12; 10:25, 27–29) Paul writes about the problem of a 'weak conscience', giving the sense that the conscience is like an organ of discernment which must make sense of the world in the light of this inner law, and can get it wrong. Aquinas took a similar view, describing conscience as the act of applying divine laws to real situations.

Particularly in the Roman Catholic Church, conscience is

primarily associated not so much with the process of discernment as with the experience of guilt, which results when the moral law is not followed. The church considers that individuals should be protected from making errors of truth, so that less emphasis is placed on an individual's conscience and more on the need to conform to the church's own moral teaching. This makes sense when you consider that this idea is allied to a strong doctrine of sin, whereby some choices will lead to the loss of saving grace or the promised eternal relationship with God. An absence of guilt led to a feeling of peace and joy, the result of a closer communion with God.

The Protestant reformers held a high view of conscience because they felt strongly that it was the responsibility of the individual to grasp faith for himself or herself, and not to rely on membership of the church as a means of salvation. Today reformed or Protestant Christians will place an emphasis on their individual relationship with Jesus as the guarantee of salvation and celebrate the promise of saving grace (that is, God's gift of forgiveness), while accepting that they will sometimes make wrong moral choices. Luther's famous saying 'sin boldly' is concerned with the idea that sin is real and unavoidable, but that this should make believers more grateful for the saving work of Jesus.[6]

This idea of the importance of (and indeed right to) an individual conscience is defended in the Universal Declaration of Human Rights, so that, for example, even in countries which have military conscription someone who is a pacifist has the right not to serve in the army. Whether influenced by religious conviction or not, where someone holds a position as a matter of conscience, this may lead to particular clarity and therefore determination to maintain a particular belief or stance regardless of its human consequences: imprisonment, torture or even death. The idea of conscience can help us to hold together the emotional and rational dimensions of ethical decision making, so that what feels right is supported by evidence that fits with the reality of the external world.

Questions

- What might be the benefits or limitations of drawing on a range of sources, such as Scripture, tradition and reason (or experience and evidence), to make ethical decisions?
- Do you think that people have duties towards each other as well as rights and responsibilities?

3
GENDER

All religions, together with belief systems such as humanism, believe that there is something special about humans in comparison to the rest of the animal kingdom. In this chapter we will try to understand not only what this might mean for all humans, but also how the differences between humans are understood. The key questions are whether difference, in particular differences in gender, are a matter of nature or nurture (culture) and whether they are of any religious or moral significance.

The Bible: made in the image of God

Christians believe that there is a special relationship between God and humanity and locate this understanding at least partially in the Genesis account of Creation.

We do not have to take the account of Creation in the Bible literally in order to consider it an important resource for thinking about what it means to be human. The stories that we tell about ourselves and about our relationship with God can, in themselves, be a testimony to God's revelation in Creation.

There are two accounts of the creation of humans in the book of Genesis. They are generally believed to originate in two different traditions in the ancient Middle East. The older tradition, dating from around the eighth century BCE, is the primary influence on the story of Creation in Genesis 2. The second, which dates from 571–486 BCE, influenced by the priestly caste, is responsible for the very ordered view of Creation in Genesis 1. It is noticeable that the compilers of the Hebrew Scripture, which was not formalised until after the time of Jesus, kept both versions of the story.

GENESIS 1:26–27

Then God said, 'Let us make humankind in our image, according to our likeness; and let them have dominion over the fish of the sea, and over the birds of the air, and over the cattle, and over all the wild animals of the earth, and over every creeping thing that creeps upon the earth.'

So God created humankind in his image, in the image of God he created them; male and female he created them.

This passage is often cited as evidence that the differences between men and women were part of God's plan for the world, followed by the deduction that the proper relationship between them is mutual desire. The Roman Catholic Church teaches, 'Everyone, man or woman, should acknowledge and accept his sexual identity. Physical, moral and spiritual difference and complementarity are orientated towards the good of marriage and the flourishing of family life.'[1] The House of Bishops in the Church of England concur: 'the division of humankind into two distinct but complementary sexes is not something accidental or evil but is, on the contrary, something good established by God himself when he first created the human race.'[2]

However, it can be argued that the position traditionally held by the church does not stand up to the critique of reason or experience and that this passage has been made to carry a weight of authority which it cannot bear.

To take the internal argument first, if we accept the authority of Genesis and agree that the way in which the first humans were created should be normative for all time, then we should all be eating a vegetarian diet, as this was clearly God's intention: 'God said, "See, I have given you every plant yielding seed that is upon the face of all the earth, and every tree with seed in its fruit; you shall have them for food"' (Genesis 1:29).

Second, we might ask, from the position of tradition, where this teaching places celibacy, which for so many years the church valued as a high calling and demanded of its priests.

Third, we might ask whether the conditions which are necessary for procreation, which might broadly be described as complementarity (at least with regard to sexual organs being capable of coming together to mingle sperm and eggs) are necessary for all humans, however necessary they are to the majority? One of the key concepts to be aware of here is the difference between what is normal and what is normative. Something that is normal can be either common, or at least not uncommon, whereas something that is normative has a moral value attached to it. So, for example, sexual activity between men and women is normal and indeed the norm (i.e. the most common expression of sexual activity) but that does not necessarily mean that it is normative, i.e. that it has a moral value.

Finally, recent developments in our understanding of gender and sexual attraction make it very clear that neither biological gender nor attraction are a simple binary, but rather that they exist on a spectrum. This is explored in more detail further on. Let's turn instead to the second description of the creation of men and women in Genesis.

GENESIS 2:18–25

Then the Lord God said, 'It is not good that the man should be alone; I will make him a helper as his partner.'

So out of the ground the Lord God formed every animal of the field and every bird of the air, and brought them to the man to see what he would call them; and whatever the man called each living creature, that was its name.

The man gave names to all cattle, and to the birds of the air, and to every animal of the field; but for the man there was not found a helper as his partner.

So the Lord God caused a deep sleep to fall upon the man, and he slept; then he took one of his ribs and closed up its place with flesh.

And the rib that the Lord God had taken from the man he made into a woman and brought her to the man.

Then the man said, 'This at last is bone of my bones and flesh of my flesh; this one shall be called Woman, for out of Man this one was taken.'

Therefore a man leaves his father and his mother and clings to his wife, and they become one flesh.

And the man and his wife were both naked and they were not ashamed.

We shouldn't miss the beautiful poetry of this passage, which is clear even in translation. The closeness between man and woman is something special and unique, something which has a different quality from the relationship between man and the rest of the animal world. The idea of shared flesh evokes a particular intimacy.

However, perhaps because of its poetic character, the passage also creates problems in interpretation. Walter Bruggemann, in his commentary on Genesis, describes this as one of the most misunderstood passages in the Bible.[3] In particular, he says that the text has been treated as decisive, when it should be seen as rather marginal. He focuses first of all on the nature of humanity in three dimensions: vocation, permission and prohibition. Humans are called to tend the Creation, given permission to enjoy it, and only finally prohibited from acquiring divine knowledge (by eating of the fruit of the tree of good and evil). Bruggemann argues that the creation of a helper for the first human must be seen in the context of this primary call. The helper cannot simply be another creature, but must be a creature of equal importance to the first human in terms of their relationship with God (not another animal over whom the first human has responsibilities).

Some people read this passage as evidence that the second creature (the woman) is a derivative, or secondary human. These readings are strongly influenced by Greek culture, which assumed that women were defective or inferior versions of men. Other readings argue that woman is the final creative touch, the fulfilment of Creation.

PHYLLIS TRIBLE ON THESE PASSAGES

Phyllis Trible is the author of two significant works in feminist biblical scholarship: *God and the Rhetoric of Sexuality* and *Texts of Terror*.[4] In 1973 she gave a groundbreaking lecture looking again at the creation of male and female in Genesis.[5] Trible takes a close look at the two passages in Genesis quoted above, paying particular attention to the Hebrew. She comes to the conclusion that humans have enjoyed companionship since they were created, but that gender division is a secondary characteristic. In other words, the primary relationship is one of companionship and not the binary relationship between the sexes.

In Genesis 2 the word used for 'man' is *adam*, which has a close relationship to the Hebrew *adamah*, meaning dust. While some read the name as the proper name for a male creature, Trible focuses on it as a generic name for all humankind. She suggests that *adam* is basically androgynous; one creature incorporating two sexes. She believes that the creature was divided in order to create a companion in the first instance, as described in Genesis 1. Humans, Trible begins, are made in God's image. Only humans receive dominion over the earth and are addressed directly. In her close reading of Genesis 1:27 Trible notes that the verse only has seven words and actually reads, 'And-created God humankind in-his-image; / in-the-image-of-God created-he *him*; / male and female created-he *them*.' 'Male and female' corresponds to 'the image of God'.

For Trible, the switch from singular to plural pronouns in the passage reveals that humanity consists of two creatures, which are both initially both male and female. 'From the beginning humankind exists as two creatures, not as one creature with double sex.' Humankind exists in a unity that is at the same time sexually differentiated. Trible characterises this as 'distinction within harmony.' Trible suggests that the division of humans into male and female was a secondary action. She quotes Genesis 2:18, in which God decides that Adam needs a 'helper fit for him', the emphasis being on the word 'helper' ('ezer' in Hebrew). Trible points out that the term 'ezer' is a relational one expressing a beneficial relationship and not one of inferiority.[6]

Man's naming of woman has also been used to justify her submissiveness, but as Trible reminds us, the Hebrew verb used when man names the animals (implying dominance) is not the same as the one used when he names woman. The text shows us male and female in a relationship of equality and mutuality prior to the Fall. While the animals created by God can be seen to be in a beneficial relationship with Adam, they are of inferior status and this inferiority is seen in the text when Adam 'names' them, thereby exercising power over them. This is not the case with woman. Instead he 'calls' her *ishshah*/woman (out of man), the rib from Adam requiring divine intervention to create into woman. She is his equal, and neither has authority over the other.

HOW SIGNIFICANT IS DIFFERENCE?

We will see throughout this book that theologians, and indeed philosophers, hold conflicting views on the importance of differences between people. While we are focused on gender, we ought to remember that such views impact on other characteristics, such as disability, race and sexuality.

In reading the passages from Genesis, if we become too closely fixated on the gender issue, we may miss the importance of the special relationship between God and all humankind, made in his image and likeness. Scripture is clear that all humans resemble God in some significant and important ways which must go beyond the capacity to create/procreate that is shared by animals, fish and birds. Irenaeus thought that people resemble God both in their natural qualities such as reason and imagination and in supernatural graces such as love and hope. They have the capacity to be holy as God is holy (Leviticus 11:44 and 1 Peter 1:16), that is to say, united with God in purpose and action. Such holiness is not predicated on anything other than being human.

A deeper unity is possible through participation in Christ, which Christians believe is gifted in the sacrament of baptism. Paul writes about this unity, between humans and Christ, in this passage from Galatians.

GALATIANS 3:28

There is no longer Jew or Greek, there is no longer slave or free, there is no longer male and female; for all of you are one in Christ Jesus.

We shall return to this passage at the end of the book. For now you might like to think about your own view of difference. Are differences between humans important, creating essential complementarity in relationships, for example, or are they irrelevant? How much is your sense of identity dependent on things which distinguish you from others? How should the world be ordered so that difference is valued but not an excuse for exploitation, power differentiation or 'othering' which leads to the exclusion of particular groups from full participation in community or society?

Questions

- What do these passages say to you about gender or sexuality?
- In what positive and negative ways have Christians used these texts?
- What was Paul meaning when he wrote to the Galatians?

Tradition: theologies of God, people and gender

God is not gendered. As God is uncreated, God does not need a gender, but our language is gendered and so our metaphors fall short of the capacity to describe God in all God's fullness. In theological terms, this aspect of God is important because, as we have seen, humanity is created in the image of God and there is a challenge to understand what is meant by this analogy.

Some richness is brought to bear by the Trinitarian nature of God, who is three persons, both distinct and separate, but interconnected and in relationship (this concept is called 'perichoresis' in classical theology, a word meaning rotation and often described in terms of a dance). Again, gendered language can get in the way of our full understanding of God as Trinity. The Creeds delineate the three persons as Father, Son and Holy Spirit and for hundreds of years the Godhead has been represented visually in masculine form – except when the Holy Spirit loses the form of a person and is shown as a dove.

Historically, in English, masculine language was deemed to be representative of all humans, and so we find the use of the word 'man' in many of our texts and hymns when humankind is intended. We have already seen how that derives from the Hebrew in the book of Genesis, where the term for 'human' is translated as 'man' and as the name of the first man, Adam. However, this universal language soon slides into something which is less inclusive, as we shall see.

Patristic theology saw Adam as the archetypal human. For Augustine this meant that the image of God was male, and the female was an inferior version of the male. Indeed, he went further, suggesting that woman alone is not made in the image of God, but only achieves that status when joined in marriage to a man. This was the understanding that prevailed the church for many centuries, although it was not the only understanding offered by the early Church Fathers.

Irenaeus thought that the only true image of God in humanity was to be found in Jesus and that humans were only ever on a journey to perfection. Clement of Alexandria thought something similar, except that humans could grow into the likeness of God by cultivating self-discipline and mastery over their passions. Gregory of Nyssa read Genesis 1:27 as a description of a non-physical, non-sexed, angelic creation which only became sexed in anticipation of the Fall. He anticipated that humanity would lose its sexual differentiation in heaven.

Whether religious teaching shaped culture, or culture shaped religious teaching, the experience of women over the centuries was shaped by the principle that they were in some way inferior to men. As a result they were denied property rights, legal rights and, frequently, access to education. It was only in the years following the Enlightenment that people began to ask more seriously about the nature of all humans, to recognise that they might have equal capacity, and to take seriously the rights of women (and slaves). As we will see, there is still a significant debate about the interplay between nature and nurture in the shaping of male and female experience and capacity, but, at least in most Western democracies women have equal legal status with men.

The use of the male pronoun as a term for all humanity began to be questioned in the mid-20th century, particularly in religious settings. Women suggested that they felt excluded by this use of language and changes were made in the texts used in many forms of worship. The recommended Biblical translation in the Church of England, the New Revised Standard Version, uses inclusive language where possible as do the liturgical texts in Common Worship. There has been a recovery of some of the biblical texts which use feminine metaphors for God, as a mother hen or a woman in labour, but they are few.

At the same time, there was a movement to incorporate the feminine into the Godhead, usually by referring to the Holy Spirit in the feminine, but also by elevating the role of Mary. One particular expression of this is found in the works of Tina Beattie, who reworks the typology of Mary as one who self-empties in order to make the flesh of Christ, and thus becomes the New Eve, the mother of the new humanity, the mother of the Body of Christ the Church.[7] Attempts to integrate the feminine into the Godhead were also influenced, for example, by Jungian theories of the feminine in the psychological makeup of both men and women.

There is a paradox arising out of feminist theology (and which is mirrored in other minority theologies): on the one hand, there is a tendency to stress the difference between men and women (or between the dominant party and the 'other'), particularly psychologically, and to argue for the recovery or integration of 'female traits' such as embodied experience, emotional intelligence and so on; on the other, there is a call for equality which downplays the difference between the genders, not only in social and economic roles, but also in the church.

Arguments about the role and person of men and women were extensively explored in the church during the debates about women's ordination. While the Church of England has come to the view that a woman can represent Christ at the altar, can teach and lead as a priest or a bishop, it has also made provision for those who do not hold these views. Thus, it is acceptable in the Church of England to believe that there is no significant distinction between men and women or to believe that there is a distinction between men and women that impacts on the roles they can play in the church. Those who believe that there is a distinction will sometimes use the language of 'complementarity', which suggests that men and women are of equal value and importance to God and in society, but that the roles for which they are intended by God are distinct and different. The language of complementarity originates in Roman Catholic teaching in the 1980s where it was used to describe the physical, moral and spiritual differences between men and women as created by God in order to enrich and order family life. This teaching asserts that the biological difference necessary for procreation is matched by other sorts of complementarity, for example in emotional or mental functioning.

Those who hold this position may develop it in one of two ways when dealing with the challenge of transgender (and gender dysphoria in people with intersex conditions). Either such conditions are treated as illnesses, causing mental distress, which can be cured through the medical intervention of hormone therapy and surgery, or they are considered God-given. In the latter case, individuals are counselled to accept the gender/sexual identity they have been given as an issue of obedience, or conformity, to the will of God, who intends men and women to exist as complementary to one another.[8]

You might notice that some of these 'essentialist' arguments were used in favour of greater inclusion of women in the church by feminist theologians. This might lead us to wonder how 'essential' our sexed bodies are to us, and whether we will retain them in heaven. The Patristic writers assumed that we would become like the angels (either all masculine, or without sexual characteristics). Others, including Ian Paul, have argued that we will retain our sexual characteristics but we will be indifferent to them, as we will be free from the desires that we associate with them.[9]

Finally, we might wonder about the purpose of gender within the community of the church. If we take the view that there are essential gender differences, then the weight that we give to those differences – in other words whether we consider that male and female characteristics and gifts are equally important to a community, or whether female characteristics are fundamentally weaker or less important than male, will impact on our views. These ideas are sometimes explored using the metaphor of the church as the body of Christ. Adrian Thatcher argues that since both Christian men and women are members of the body of Christ, the body of Christ is androgynous.[10] Graham Ward takes this idea further, noting that Jesus' body is not like other bodies, because of special phenomena such as the virgin birth, transfiguration, presence in the Eucharist, crucifixion, resurrection and ascension. He suggests that the body of Jesus has fluidity which puts it beyond gender.[11] We will return to these ideas at the end of this book, but for now let's just consider what the church teaches about difference and hospitality.

I CORINTHIANS 12:12–26

For just as the body is one and has many members, and all the members of the body, though many, are one body, so it is with Christ.

For in the one Spirit we were all baptized into one body – Jews or Greeks, slaves or free – and we were all made to drink of one Spirit.

Indeed, the body does not consist of one member but of many.

If the foot were to say, 'Because I am not a hand, I do not belong to the body,' that would not make it any less a part of the body.

And if the ear were to say, 'Because I am not an eye, I do not belong to the body,' that would not make it any less a part of the body.

If the whole body were an eye, where would the hearing be? If the whole body were hearing, where would the sense of smell be?

But as it is, God arranged the members in the body, each one of them, as he chose.

If all were a single member, where would the body be?

As it is, there are many members, yet one body.

The eye cannot say to the hand, 'I have no need of you,' nor again the head to the feet, 'I have no need of you.'

On the contrary, the members of the body that seem to be weaker are indispensable,

and those members of the body that we think less honourable we clothe with greater honour, and our less respectable members are treated with greater respect;

whereas our more respectable members do not need this. But God has so arranged the body, giving the greater honour to the inferior member,

that there may be no dissension within the body, but the members may have the same care for one another.

If one member suffers, all suffer together with it; if one member is honoured, all rejoice together with it.

When St Paul writes of the church as a single body, he pays particular attention to the inclusion of the parts that might be seen to be inferior or less than others. Indeed, he insists that they are of equal worth and importance. We can read this passage as an exhortation to inclusion. However, we also need to consider what it means to include those with whom we disagree, in other parts of the church for example.

The theme of welcome and hospitality appears often in the Bible. We can see times when the people of God have been very aware of an imperative to welcome others: particularly in the story of Abraham and the welcome to the three strangers at Mamre, when he finds that he has 'entertained angels unawares' (Genesis 18) and in the repeated calls in the law of Leviticus to offer support to widows, orphans and strangers in the land.

Jesus is portrayed as continuously seeking out the marginalised in the community: women and children, the sick or dying, tax collectors, sex workers and foreigners. Christians might see this as a call to challenge their prejudices and biases to offer a welcome to all, and in this instance, to offer a welcome to those who may be excluded because they do not fit our conventional expectations in the expression of their gender.

Many Christians see the existence of the small number of people who do not fit the usual binary gender categories as morally neutral. It may be helpful here just to identify the difference between those who are intersex and those who identify as transgender. In the first case, described in more detail below, the person is born with a gender-atypical body and may make a choice to identify either as male, female or neither and to accompany this decision with medical intervention, or not. In the second case, someone who is born with the sexual characteristics of one gender experiences strong identification with the other and may choose to have surgery to create the physical characteristics (for example, penis and facial hair or vagina and breasts) of their new gender. People with intersex conditions may accept the gender assigned to them at birth, or chose to reassign their gender. The Church of England does not legally discriminate against people who have gone through gender reassignment and accepts and welcomes them as not only lay people but as clergy. They are free to marry a person of a different gender to their assigned gender, despite the fact that sexual activity within such marriages cannot lead to the procreation of children.

The experience of transgender Christians can be helpful in reminding us of the extent to which gender is linked to our sense of self before God. Those who have grown up feeling alienated from their bodies often describe the way in which their sense of self, and their relationship with God, is put right through surgical intervention that allows them to inhabit a body which is a physical mirror of their psychological gender identity. The destruction of a body and the history which accompanies it, in order to be reshaped into a new body and a new identity, is a profoundly serious business. Rachel Mann, a transgender priest, has written of 'killing' her former self, while others acknowledge the mystery involved in 'reaching wholeness through mutilation'.[12]

Reason: gender and science

Some of us learned in school that sex chromosomes determine the sex of a baby. Two X chromosomes make a girl, XY make a boy. We now know that life is not that simple. Today we know that the various elements of what we consider 'male' and 'female' don't always line up neatly, with all the XXs – complete with ovaries, vagina, oestrogen, female gender identity and feminine behaviour – on one side and all the XYs – testes, penis, testosterone, male gender identity and masculine behaviour – on the other. It's possible to be XX and mostly male in terms of anatomy, physiology and psychology, just as it's possible to be XY and mostly female. Each embryo starts out with a pair of primitive organs, the proto-gonads, which develop into male or female gonads at about six to eight weeks. Sex differentiation is usually set in motion by a gene on the Y chromosome, the SRY gene, which makes the proto-gonads turn into testes. The testes then secrete testosterone and other male hormones, and the foetus develops a prostate, scrotum and penis. Without the SRY gene, the proto-gonads become ovaries that secrete oestrogen, and the foetus develops female anatomy (uterus, vagina and clitoris).

But the SRY gene's function isn't always straightforward. The gene might be missing or dysfunctional, leading to an XY embryo that fails to develop male anatomy and is identified at birth as a girl. Or it might show up on the X chromosome, leading to an XX embryo that develops male anatomy and is identified at birth as a boy.

Genetic variations can occur that are unrelated to the SRY gene, such as complete androgen insensitivity syndrome (CAIS), in which an XY embryo's cells respond minimally, if at all, to the signals of male hormones. Even though the proto-gonads become testes and the foetus produces androgens, external male genitals don't develop. The baby looks female, with a clitoris and vagina, and in most cases will grow up feeling herself to be a girl. Which gender is this baby, then? Is she the girl she believes herself to be? Or, because of her XY chromosomes – not to mention the testes in her abdomen – is she 'really' male?

Scientists now recognise three different factors that influence gender: biology, gender identification and gender expression. In the majority of people all three line up and fit in to one of the binary categories, i.e. male or female. These people are known as cisgender. The percentage of those who identify in non-cisgender ways is thought to be about 3 per cent (this is not related to their sexuality, which we will discuss later in this chapter).

BIOLOGICAL SEX

Sex determination exists on a spectrum, with genitals, chromosomes, gonads and hormones all playing a role. Most people's sexual characteristics fit into the male or female category, and the percentage of those with ambiguous characteristics is usually considered to be between 0.05 per cent and 1.7 per cent of the population.[13] These folk are usually called intersex and in the early part of the 20th century were often assigned gender at birth, followed by surgical intervention to give them the outward signs of that gender. This treatment is no longer recommended, and parents are encouraged to live with uncertainty until the child is old enough for the family to make a collective decision about hormonal or surgical intervention.

GENDER IDENTIFICATION

Gender self-identification includes a sense of personal identity and identification with others of the same gender. Generally children have established this by the age of three, but they may go on experimenting with different roles and costumes for longer. Where individuals self-identify with a gender that is different from their biological sex, particularly during and after puberty, they may be transgender and seek to have the outward signs of their gender changed. Although there has been a lot of publicity about this condition in recent years, it is very rare and significant care needs to be taken before hormone treatments and surgery are considered.

GENDER EXPRESSION

People express gender through clothing, behaviour, language and other outward signs. Whether these attributes are labelled masculine or feminine varies among cultures. Gender expression is also manipulated and encouraged by commercial interests, for example in the provision of highly gender-specific clothing and toys for children.

People who choose not to express their gender strongly through clothing, behaviour or language are sometimes labelled androgynous or third gender. Third gender can include anatomical males who behave in a feminine manner and are sexually attracted to men. More rarely, some third-gender people, such as the burnesha of Albania or the fa'afatama of Samoa, are anatomical females who live in a masculine manner.

There are such people all over the world: South Asia (hijra), Nigeria (yan daudu), Mexico (muxe), Samoa (fa' afafine), Thailand (kathoey), Tonga (fakaleiti), Hawaii (mahu), Native American (two spirit). In some cultures third-gender people are believed to play a special role in the community, which may have a spiritual dimension. In other cultures any diversity from non-binary gender expression may be strongly discouraged and considered immoral or unnatural.

Even if you consider the expectations of schools and businesses with regard to the wearing of uniform, you can see how what is normative can become defined as 'normal', and defying these expectations easily appears as a form of rebellion or transgression. An example in the Western world would be the phenomenon of drag queens: men who adopt exaggerated and sexualised expressions of female clothing and makeup.

GENDER FLUIDITY

One thing to be aware of is the very different way in which issues of gender are seen by a younger generation. A recent survey of a thousand young people, aged 18 to 34, in the United States found that half of them think that 'Gender is a spectrum, and some people fall outside conventional categories.' Fifty per cent of respondents also self-identified as being outside the conventional categories.[14]

Questions

- What is your experience of gender identity?
- How comfortable are you with the idea that gender is fluid?
- How should the church treat those who do not conform to gender stereotypes, or experience their gender atypically?

4
DESIRE

At the heart of a sexual relationship is the experience of mutual desire, the rush of emotions and physiological responses felt by both partners. But sexual desire is not the only kind of desire; we have emotional and physical longings for food, for security and for self-worth. As we noted in the Introduction, it is not possible to detach these emotional and physical responses from our intellectual or rational lives. The questions which philosophers and theologians have asked about desire concern the relationship between desire and goodness, and between desire and the will.

Some are wary of desire, believing that the emotional and physical motivations that shape desire actually disable the will, or distort it. Others welcome desire as a driver towards the good, the true and the pure. In this chapter we will examine the place of desire; the role of the law or conscience in modifying or controlling desire; and the character of immoral desire.

Desire: the Bible

THE OLD TESTAMENT

In order to understand the special place of sexual desire in the Old Testament, we need to know a little about the culture of the ancient Near East and the religions surrounding early Judaism. In these cultures, the gods were sexual beings and intercourse between gods and humans was one way in which the fertility of the land, crops, animals and people was ensured. Sexual activity between gods and humans was sometimes mirrored in forms of religious sexual activity, for example the use of temple prostitutes.

By contrast, Jewish Scripture tells us that Adam and Eve are created in the image of God, but they are not gods. There is an important and significant distinction between God and God's creatures. When people forget this and seek divine powers, by eating of the tree of knowledge, or by aspiring to reach the divine heights of heaven by building a tower in Babel, they are punished. This different approach may explain the lack of positive theology or poetry about sexual desire in Jewish Scripture, though, as we shall see, it is not entirely absent.

Humans are given the capacity to procreate as a gift through which they can serve God in his purpose, by making the world a fruitful place. For the people who shaped the Old Testament, sexual activity neither makes humans divine, nor is it intended to be an interaction between humans and divine creatures. However, it is a good thing and God makes men and women desire one another so that they are drawn together in companionship and support. As we have seen in Chapter 3, scholars disagree about whether or not men and women should be seen as of equal status in God's eyes in their innocent state, and they equally disagree about the place of desire in the Garden of Eden (that is, in the unsullied human state). As we shall see, the character of desire was fundamentally changed following the incident in which Eve, and then Adam, ate the fruit from the tree of knowledge. God found them in the garden, and punished them by banishing them from Eden, and by changing the relationship between them.

GENESIS 3:16–19

To the woman he said, 'I will greatly increase your pangs in childbearing; in pain you shall bring forth children, yet your desire shall be for your husband, and he shall rule over you.'

And to the man he said, 'Because you have listened to the voice of your wife, and have eaten of the tree about which I commanded you, "You shall not eat of it," cursed is the ground because of you; in toil you shall eat of it all the days of your life;

thorns and thistles it shall bring forth for you; and you shall eat the plants of the field.

By the sweat of your face you shall eat bread until you return to the ground, for out of it you were taken; you are dust, and to dust you shall return.'

All theologians agree that after humans have disobeyed God, the roles of men and women are distinguished; Eve is told that she will experience pain in childbirth, and that while she will still desire her husband he will rule over her. At the same time, Adam will now toil and sweat to make the earth bring forth food to eat. We commonly call these events 'The Fall' although this term is not present in the biblical account. There is a sense that people have fallen out of favour with God, or fallen from grace (that is, God's unconditional love), after eating from the tree of the knowledge of good and evil. Life becomes painful and difficult, and sexual desire is placed in the context of this situation of striving and sorrow.

But life is not without its comforts and compensations. As we read through the Old Testament we find people in loving relationships and happy families. Sexual desire is boundaried and regulated through marriage, and sex within marriage is regulated by purity laws which forbid intercourse at certain times, for example during menstruation. There are examples of transgressive desire being punished, as when David seduces Bathsheba (2 Samuel 11), the wife of his military commander, and the resulting child dies. On the other hand, God does not appear to punish Abraham for attempting to prostitute his wife to protect his own life (Genesis 12), but rather punishes the Egyptian pharaoh who has accepted this woman as a gift. This is just one example of a relationship in which a woman is exploited by her husband. In trying to make sense of the human relationships in the

Old Testament we often seem to be faced with patriarchal cultural norms rather than images of God's preferred models of relationship for men and women. Instead, we find that image in the theme, which runs through the Old Testament, of God's desire for his people.

Time and again God demonstrates his love by returning to the people who have betrayed their promise to worship him alone and to follow his laws. This motif of desire is particularly apparent in the story of the prophet Hosea. Hosea is told to marry a prostitute and to love her faithfully despite her unfaithfulness to him. We are expected to understand that this relationship is a mirror of God's love and desire for God's people. Not only is the language of marriage and covenant used to describe the relationship between God and the people, but the people's betrayal (frequently by turning to worship the Canaanite god Baal) is likened to adultery. God sets out to seduce Israel in order to bring her back into a relationship of love.

The clearest description of physical desire can be found in the Song of Songs, one of the books of the Bible supposedly written by King Solomon, one of the foundational figures of the Jewish nation. The Song of Songs is a poem, full of beautiful images celebrating sexual desire, intimacy and love. In it, the lovers celebrate one another's bodies in extravagant metaphors: breasts like twin gazelles, clusters of dates or grapes; cheeks like pomegranates; hair like flocks of goats. The Patristic scholars were content to accept this extravagance as long as it could be understood as an allegory (a parallel) to God's love for his people or, in Christianity, of Christ's love for the church. However, it can also be read as an affirmation of embodied sexual human love, perhaps between the king and his wife, or simply between any man and woman. Allegorical readings make most sense if we acknowledge that desire itself can be a good thing, helping us to understand something about God. As we will see later, thinking in this way can lead to the further expectation that human desire and the experience of physical love can open people up to an experience of the love of God.

THE NEW TESTAMENT

We will look in detail at Jesus' view of marriage in Chapter 6. For the present it is worth noting that while he seems to have a positive view of marriage, he was himself unmarried. Some scholars see this as significant, arguing that it was highly unusual for a man in his thirties in first-century Palestine to remain unmarried. Jesus himself makes no reference to singleness and does not say that it is a preferential form of life, although, as we shall see, the church later imposed this form of life on clergy for many centuries.

St Paul's attitude to sexual desire appears distinctly negative, but we need to understand this in the context of two important factors. The first is that Paul was writing his letters in response to particular pastoral crises in the early church. That means that the majority of his writing about sex focuses on occasions where it has gone wrong. Second, Paul was focused on spreading the gospel as quickly as possible, especially because he was expecting the return of Christ and the end of time within a generation. In these circumstances, it is best for people to remain single, without family ties, and single-minded about the gospel, and only to marry as a last resort.

TRADITION: THEOLOGIES OF DESIRE

In understanding the purpose of desire in Creation, theologians have generally asked why God would have given humans the capacity to desire and what its proper end or *telos* should be. Sexual desire is necessary for the procreation of children and so is morally linked to a goal or *telos* of childbirth and child rearing. We have seen how this idea is linked to the task of sharing in God's creative activity, through the procreation of children. As we shall see, this has implications for the way in which marriage is understood as something different from all other categories of human relationship. There are theologians, like Augustine, who are thoroughly suspicious of desire and treat it as a nasty consequence of our sinful natures. Desire is seen as something which needs to be mastered or disciplined, rather than something that contributes to our sense of wellbeing, or drives us towards anything good. There are expressions of spirituality that are suspicious of any expression of desire, Christian stoicism or asceticism for example, and some influential Christian teachers who clearly had a distrust or even disgust of sexual desire, or were simply misogynist. A subtler form of thinking is to suggest that desire has been corrupted by the Fall and we cannot experience it in its uncorrupted pure form in this life. Luther cheerfully accepted that desire is a reality for sinful humanity and was a keen supporter of marriage for that reason.

However, a richer and more nuanced understanding of desire places it within a broader context, in which all of our desires derive from a fundamental desire for God. We can see that sexual desire, which participates in God's creativity, is a wonderful expression of that desire, but there are other ways in which human desires can reflect the divine nature. For example, desire for someone else's company that is self-giving, whether expressed in a physical sexual relationship or a sacrificial self-giving in friendship, parenthood or caring, might give us a feeling for the self-sacrificial desire that the Son of God, Jesus, felt for humanity, or that God the Father felt for his Son. The whole character of the Christian God, who is both three and one, in relationship may tell us something about the *telos* or purpose of desire, which leads to love.

Notwithstanding these ideas, we will need to ask whether *all* expressions of desire are morally neutral or morally good, and if not, on what basis Christians might make choices about the desires on which they act.

It is often suggested that the Christian view of desire has been thoroughly distorted by Greek philosophy, and in particular that of Platonism with its dualism between the spiritual and the physical – between soul and body. Many people have argued that Old Testament theology is one in which body and spirit cannot be divided, but that Platonic dualism led to an unfortunate dualism in Christian thought. A particularly strong and pervasive influence is the thought of Augustine of Hippo. Augustine seems to have had a personal problem with controlling his lust, and his anxiety about lust has permeated much of the teaching against sexual desire in the Western Church.[1] Augustine argued that the only legitimate end or *telos* of desire is God, and that desire should only be expressed spiritually through the longing for God in prayer. Physical desire is simply a poor substitute for the desire for God and the highest ideal would be celibacy, whereby there is no substitution and no experience of fulfilled desire in the body.

Augustine thought there was sin in sex because he thought of sex fundamentally in spiritual terms. Augustine conceded that before the Fall sexual intercourse could have been pleasurable without being the cause of sin, although he tended to conclude that humans took no pleasure in sex before the Fall. He imagined Adam and Eve engaging in intercourse without any expression of feeling or desire. By contrast, he believed that in our fallen state humans are incapable of having sex without experiencing selfish desire, pride, greed or lust. Augustine suggested that one of the consequences of the Fall was that men no longer had control of their bodies, and could experience desire (an erection, for example) or impotence (the inability to get an erection), which was not related to their will or intention.

Augustine became associated with the idea that original sin (that is, inherent sinfulness) was transmitted through sexual intercourse and that, as a consequence, all children were born sinful and in need of salvation. Thus, even sex for the sake of procreation was a necessary evil and not a good thing. Avoidance of sex, i.e. celibacy, was much to be preferred.

For much of the Middle Ages celibacy was the ideal in the church, having been made compulsory for clergy in the fourth century. The origins of priestly celibacy are likely to be connected to the need for purity prior to celebrating the Eucharist (a practice which would have its origins in the need for priestly purity prior to ritual sacrifice). Beyond the fact that clerical celibacy functioned as a spiritual discipline, it also was guarantor of the independence of the church in an age when marriage was frequently used as a tool of political, social or financial power. As we've already noted, the idea of celibacy was routinely flouted, particularly among the leaders of the church: at least four popes during the Renaissance period fathered children and conferred titles on them.

In our own time, the vocation to celibacy as a positive lifestyle choice has been undermined by a number of factors. The first might be the assumption that celibacy requires the unhealthy suppression of natural sexual desire and so is psychologically unhealthy. Sexual activity is a sign of maturity and so is something to be sought, whereas virginity is associated with a childish, even embarrassing state.

The second is the widespread awareness of sexual abuse of others by clergy or religious who were nominally celibate, in particular in the Roman Catholic Church, but also among Anglican celibate clergy, monks and nuns.

The third is the confusion between celibacy and singleness. In our sexualised society many relationships of mutual companionship are assumed by those outside them to be sexually active, when they may in fact be celibate.

In recent times, where people without religious views have embraced celibacy it has often been because they have experienced unhealthy sexual relationships in the past, seek to reject the imbalance of power in male/female relationships, or feel the need to get out of the 'dating game' for a period of time because they have found it stressful trying to find and maintain sexual relationships.

There is little evidence in the general culture of the once widespread idea that you might 'save yourself' for that special person, or even for your wedding night. It could be argued that sexual intercourse has become the gateway to a more serious relationship, rather than the culmination of courtship. You might want to consider whether this change has devalued the way in which people think about sexual activity or sexual intercourse, which many Christians would believe to be a special gift in Creation. One reason they might think that relates to the idea that sexual desire is an analogy for the desire for God, and sexual experience an analogy for union with God.

DESIRE AND SPIRITUALITY

There is a strong tradition within Christian spirituality of eroticism in prayer, which is associated with a willingness to surrender to God completely, just as partners in sexual intercourse surrender to one another in their passion. You can see this surrender in Bernini's famous carving of Theresa of Avila. In the sculpture, the saint is being pierced in her heart by a golden arrow held in the hand of an angel and her face, with its open mouth and half-closed eyes, is clearly consumed in ecstasy. Theresa described the sweetness of surrender to God as being both spiritual and physical.[2]

There is another description of self-abasement or surrender to God in John Donne's poem 'Batter My Heart' which concludes:

> *Take me to you, imprison me, for I*
> *Except you enthrall me, never shall be free,*
> *Nor ever chaste, except you ravish me.*

There is very little research into the relationship between spiritual desire and its physical expression, and that which exists is ambivalent.[3] However, there is no doubt that Theresa and John Donne are describing highly charged emotional experiences, which remind us that the desire for God is never an entirely intellectual exercise. Whether desire is to be encouraged or disciplined, it engages both our hearts and bodies. For this reason, Christians will practise holy habits of the body as well as the mind, which may include forms of denial – fasting, silence, solitude – not only as a means of disciplining the will, but also as a means of opening the self up to God. There is some evidence that abstaining from sex or deferring it will actually improve the experience when it occurs.

Neither the Bible nor Augustine is alone in suggesting that sexual desire needs controlling and reining in. The philosophers of the Enlightenment, particularly Kant, were suspicious of emotion and preferred to focus on the will as the organ of intellectual choice. Too much enthusiasm, they argued, prevents us from making wise decisions and may lead to rash actions. Before reliable birth control, this would certainly have been true, since prematurely engaging in sexual activity could lead to unwanted pregnancy, for example. However, it can be argued that Kant and Descartes focused too exclusively on the mind or the will, and imagined that all aspects of life can simply be ruled by rational intellectual decision making.[4]

In modern times, initially influenced by Freud, and with a much more sophisticated understanding of the way in which our brains and bodies work, it has been realised that you can't separate out emotions and desires from the intellect. This may help us to see both that disciplining desire is quite difficult and requires practice (and social norms in society which help to create expectations about behaviour), and that paying attention to our bodies may also help us to understand what we are thinking or how we are likely to behave.

It might also help us to recognise how sex becomes distorted by other desires: the desire for admiration, for power, or to fit in to a culture or friendship group, for example. We will look at the way in which desire can be affected by social and cultural considerations, including, for example, its use in advertising, in the section Reason and desire: science and ethics below.

Questions

- How do you understand desire and desire for God?
- What should the church say about desire and self-control?

Reason and desire: science and ethics

In the relatively recent past, a sexual relationship was seen as the culmination of a romantic relationship and sexual desire as something that would be enhanced by being disciplined, at least for a while, before being fulfilled. This view was undoubtedly influenced by cultural Christianity, but also by the need to avoid unwanted pregnancy. It seems as if the idea of 'saving yourself' for the right person, or abstaining from sexual activity in the early stages of a romantic relationship, have largely disappeared from people's thinking.

This change, at least in people's behaviour in the Western world, has been partly brought about by the availability of contraception, which has separated sexual activity from the likelihood of pregnancy and the responsibilities which might be associated with parenthood. On the other hand, research into promiscuity (defined as casual sex with a number of partners) seems to suggest that for the majority of people there is still a strong link between the desire for sex and the desire for companionship and a life partner. Although there is anxiety that promiscuity will lead to unwanted consequences including teenage pregnancy and the increase of sexually transmitted disease, the evidence for this is not conclusive.[5]

Recent research, in particular by Helen Fisher and her colleagues, has shown how the elements of desire, which she characterises as lust, romantic love and attachment, are connected in our brain chemistry. She has shown how not only lust, but romantic love, produce changes in the most primitive part of our brain, the reptilian or limbic system, over which we have no conscious control. Romantic love creates feelings of craving for another person, which becomes addictive. The dopamine rush which their company produces quickly needs to be topped up with more contact, and still more! However, she has also shown that the cravings increase when you can't get what you want, so that the dopamine rush is increased after an absence of the loved one. Second, and perhaps with consequences for our moral or ethical behaviour, she demonstrates that although casual sex can be separated from romantic love, orgasm creates chemical reactions which stimulate the areas of the brain associated with romantic love and attachment. Fisher suggests that we are biologically hard wired to connect sexual pleasure with romantic love and attachment. We might also wonder whether her research implies that delayed gratification actually improves or enhances the qualities of a relationship, including building up the attachment (i.e. staying power) within the relationship.[6]

Whatever the personal and social value of stable relationships, we might also want to ask about the quality of the relationship for the individuals within it. The ethics of personal relationships in the Western Enlightenment tradition have been heavily influenced by Kant's development of the Universal or Golden Rule. Kant suggested that we should understand the teaching to love our neighbour as ourselves to mean that we should treat others as 'an end in themselves' – that is, that we should not use them for our own ends.

Humanity, for Kant, is an individual's rational nature and capacity for rational choice. The characteristic feature of humanity is an individual's capacity for rationally setting and pursuing his or her own ends. A being with humanity is capable of deciding what is valuable, and of finding ways to realise and promote this value. Humanity is what is special about human beings. It distinguishes them from animals and inanimate objects. Because human beings are special in this sense they have, unlike animals and objects, a *dignity* (an 'inner worth', as opposed to a 'relative worth').[7] It is crucial, for Kant, that each person respects humanity in others, as well as humanity in their own person. Humanity must never be treated merely as a means, but always at the same time as an end.[8]

This way of looking at other people can offer a way of challenging the ethics of desire, without suggesting that desire in itself is a bad thing. To desire another person, to be sexually aroused by their presence, to experience longing for their body, when such feelings are linked to the desire also to give that person pleasure, to share the experience of self-giving with them, would be to treat them as an end in themselves. Such sensitivity requires good communication and an understanding of the other, especially perhaps of the different ways in which men and women experience and enjoy sexual activity and come to climax. But Kant's definition does not only apply in the setting of an actual physical relationship, but also in the way in which people become the objects of one another's gaze.

When the gaze is entirely for the benefit of the onlooker, by Kant's definition the object of desire is being used, the person has become a tool or instrument for the arousal of another. This idea was developed by feminists in the 1970s into another concept, that of objectification, as a critique of pornography. Pornography has always been extremely difficult to define. The Greek word *porneia* (as used by St Paul) can mean almost any kind of sex outside marriage, so there is some implication of transgressive sex involved, but it has not proved easy to define pornography except according to social norms.

What feminism has helpfully highlighted is that images intended to provoke desire always entail consumption, specifically consumption of the weaker by the more powerful. It is argued particularly in the case of photography and film that pornography reduces humans simply to bodies, or even body parts, without autonomy or agency.

But where are the boundaries? Throughout history people have created images of idealised and beautiful humans to admire. Many of these images – think of the Venus de Milo, or Rodin's 'Kiss' – have been intended to inspire thoughts of purity, beauty and truth. On the other hand, numerous advertisements for perfume, aftershave or underwear have used beautiful bodies to attract our attention and arouse our desire, in order to sell us a product. Levels of undress, sexualised movements and simulated sexual activity that would have been considered pornographic less than two generations ago are now normal fare in our Saturday night television viewing. The internet has made pornography widely available to young people at a time when they are working out their own sexuality and beginning real sexual relationships, while an older generation find it more difficult to articulate an ethical approach to desire which is not coloured by cultural moral norms.

The flip side of objectification by others is the need for external validation of our own bodies. Both young men and young women seek approval of their physique and fashion style or image choices through social media and there is some evidence that this is the cause of increasing anxiety and unhappiness.

Desire is not just a physical symptom related to sex (whatever our misreading of Freud might suggest) but a response to all sorts of stimuli. Just as we can desire an ice cream, and be sold ice cream as if it were a sexual object, so we can be sexually attracted to someone because of their intellect, their money or their power. Desire for power is often distorted into sexual exploitation, as has been highlighted by recent media campaigns. The 2013 National Survey of Sexual Attitudes and Lifestyle (Natsal-3) found that 9.8 per cent of women and 1.4 per cent of men had been forced to have sex against their will.[9]

Finally, we might return to the problem of the will and desire. We all know the difference between the way we would like to behave and the way we actually behave, whether that relates to eating, being less selfish, or sticking to an exercise plan. From St Paul to Freud, we can find thinkers puzzling over the reality that we can find ourselves doing things that rationally we don't want to do. Contemporary neuroscience has helped us to understand how the different parts of our brain are implicated in this problem. Our ancient, animal brain (what scientists call the limbic area, and what Steve Peters has called our 'inner chimp') kicks in quickly and effortlessly when presented with stimuli like food, sex or threat.[10] Our human rational brain, the prefrontal cortex, works much more slowly and requires much more energy. Many of our desires, including our sexual desires, are driven by the quicker-acting animal part of our brain, and so can run away with us before we have made a conscious decision to act on them. In most situations we have schooled our brains through repetition and habit, so that we don't grab food from someone else at the bus stop, however delicious their doughnut looks! But if we apply this knowledge to other forms of desire, we might begin to consider how and in what way sexual desire should be schooled.

In the past, society set boundaries around sexual desire through the institution of marriage, and we will turn to this in Chapter 6, when we will also ask about the characteristics of marriage which could be found in other relationships.

Questions

- Can you think of some ways in which desire is disordered in our society?
- You might also consider the ways in which desire is most often disordered in your own life...
- What does good/virtuous sex look like?

5
SAME-SEX DESIRE

Desire for another person of the same sex is a particular problem for the church, and for this reason, I have separated out the issue into this additional chapter. In some ways, this might distort the argument, as many people will want to argue that the ethical questions that face individuals whose sexuality falls outside the heterosexual norm are identical to those of their straight sisters and brothers. However, I want to honour the views of those who see the world very differently and to recognise the enormous and rapid changes in society which have taken place in the past fifty to a hundred years, hence the need for a more expansive discussion of this topic.

The Bible and same-sex desire

For hundreds of years people have assumed that the Bible was unequivocal in its condemnation of sexual activity between people of the same gender. A 'commonsense' reading of Genesis 19, Leviticus 18:22 and 20:13, Romans 1:26–27, 2 Corinthians 6:9 and 1 Timothy 1:10 (the so-called 'clobber texts') seemed clear and uncontentious. The Roman Catholic Church continues to hold this view, stating in its catechesis, 'Sacred scripture presents homosexual acts as acts of grave depravity.'[1] As social attitudes have changed, some Biblical scholars have reviewed these texts and some have come to rather different conclusions about their significance and relevance as teaching for

Christians today. There are a number of approaches that can be taken, and as you might expect, all are contested:

- It can be argued that these few passages are more ambiguous and harder to translate than is usually acknowledged. This approach has been particularly adopted with regard to the writings of St Paul, where he occasionally seems to create a new word, or use an existing Greek word in a new way.
- It can be argued that all the passages relate to specific contexts and do not refer to an overarching category of people or activity. It is certainly true that there was no such category as a homosexual person until the label was used first in medical texts in the 19th century, and there is a significant problem in describing and interpreting behaviour within cultures which are very different from our own.
- It can be argued that we should be highly attuned to the nature of gender relationships in the cultural settings in which both the Old and New Testaments were written. The insights of feminist readings of biblical texts may help us to read with a more critical eye towards cultural norms.
- Finally, and perhaps most importantly, these texts need to be read alongside other teachings on sexual morality, particularly the teaching of Jesus and St Paul on celibacy, and in the context of the overarching messages of salvation in the gospel.

THE OLD TESTAMENT

GENESIS 19:1–8 AND 24–25

The two angels came to Sodom in the evening, and Lot was sitting in the gateway of Sodom. When Lot saw them, he rose to meet them, and bowed down with his face to the ground.

He said, 'Please, my lords, turn aside to your servant's house and spend the night, and wash your feet; then you can rise early and go on your way.' They said, 'No; we will spend the night in the square.'

But he urged them strongly; so they turned aside to him and entered his house; and he made them a feast, and baked unleavened bread, and they ate.

But before they lay down, the men of the city, the men of Sodom, both young and old, all the people to the last man, surrounded the house;

and they called to Lot, 'Where are the men who came to you tonight? Bring them out to us, so that we may know them.'

Lot went out of the door to the men, shut the door after him,

and said, 'I beg you, my brothers, do not act so wickedly.

Look, I have two daughters who have not known a man; let me bring them out to you, and do to them as you please; only do nothing to these men, for they have come under the shelter of my roof.'

Then the Lord rained on Sodom and Gomorrah sulphur and fire from the Lord out of heaven;

and he overthrew those cities, and all the Plain, and all the inhabitants of the cities, and what grew on the ground.

This story from Genesis describing the 'sin of Sodom' is the source of the term 'sodomy', meaning anal intercourse. A crowd of men turns up at the door of Lot's house where he is entertaining strangers, and demands to 'know' them. This is the same word used when Noah 'knows' his daughters who subsequently become pregnant – so it clearly denotes penetrative sex. We might conclude that the men of Sodom are being condemned for their attempt at homosexual rape, and that Lot's offer of his daughters is an attempt to replace the disordered objects of desire with a more acceptable one. But, in truth, this interpretation dates from the late Middle Ages, when the crime of the men of Sodom was condemned by Thomas Aquinas, along with all forms of sex which were not open to the procreation of children.

Before Thomas, the crime of the men of Sodom was primarily understood as one of inhospitality to strangers. This is much clearer when we read the passage in the light of the story which leads into this one – which is the tale of Abraham and Sarah entertaining three men by the oak of Mamre (Genesis 18). In that case, Abraham defers to the strangers, offers them food and drink, and only then discovers that they are messengers sent by God (in other words angels). Lot, Abraham's nephew, shows the same hospitality, bowing before the strangers and offering them shelter and food. This behaviour is in marked contrast to the lack of hospitality shown by the people of Sodom towards the same strangers.

Drawing on this passage in his own teaching, Jesus tells his disciples to shake the dust from their feet when their message is not welcome, for these towns will be judged like the city of Sodom for their lack of hospitality to God's messengers (Matthew 10:5–15).

The act of homosexual rape can be understood in this incident as an abuse of power and a disordering of the natural hierarchy, rather than a disorder of desire. In a society in which penetrative sex indicated rights of possession, primarily a man's possession of his wife, it was symbolic of a power relationship. The one who is penetrated is the inferior partner in an asymmetric relationship. Guests should be given a place of honour and not treated as inferior, hence the seriousness of the crime committed by the men of Sodom.

We ought not to gloss over Lot's offer of his virgin daughters to the men of Sodom, as this reinforces the cultural reality that permeates the Old Testament. Lot's daughters are his possessions and he is free to dispense with them as he pleases. For this reason, he can offer them in place of his guests, to serve the men of Sodom. While this may sound abhorrent to us, within his own culture this act reinforces the idea that Lot is offering incredibly costly hospitality to his guests, since the value of his daughters will be diminished by the loss of their virginity once they have been used to protect the honour of the visitors.

LEVITICUS 18:22 AND 20:13

You shall not lie with a male as with a woman; it is an abomination.

If a man lies with a male as with a woman, both of them have committed an abomination; they shall be put to death; their blood is upon them.

These passages come from the so-called 'Holiness Codes' of the Book of Leviticus, which contain lists of prohibitions for the people of God, gathered over three centuries and codified in the exilic period, when the Jews were held captive in Babylon. The codes were intended to help maintain the purity of the Jews, in particular to do so in distinction from the other communities around them. The theme of distinctiveness and separation runs through many of the commands; for example, there are prohibitions on the wearing of mixed fibres, of planting mixtures of seeds, and of intermarriage. The order of things, including the hierarchical ordering of nature and of the roles of men and women, underlies many of these prohibitions. Thus we can see that, once again, a specific act that distorts the hierarchy between men and women, because it requires a man to take the subordinate role, is being prohibited.

While many people assume that these passages are dealing with 'gay sex', it can be argued that what we read here equates simply to sexual penetration. Neither of these passages simply refer to 'sleeping with' or even mutual sexual stimulation, but only to anal penetration.

THE NEW TESTAMENT

I CORINTHIANS 6:9–10

Do you not know that wrongdoers will not inherit the kingdom of God? Do not be deceived! Fornicators, idolaters, adulterers, male prostitutes [malakoi], sodomites [arsenokoites],

thieves, the greedy, drunkards, revilers, robbers – none of these will inherit the kingdom of God.

I TIMOTHY I:9–10

This means understanding that the law is laid down not for the innocent but for the lawless and disobedient, for the godless and sinful, for the unholy and profane, for those who kill their father or mother, for murderers,

fornicators, sodomites [arsenokoites], slave traders, liars, perjurers, and whatever else is contrary to the sound teaching.

Of the two words which appear in Paul's list of vices, one, *malakoi*, is a Greek word which literally means 'soft' and can be applied not only to the passive partners in a sexual encounter but any form of luxury, soft living or self-indulgence. The second, *arsenokoites*, is a neologism from Paul, literally meaning 'male-bedder'. There was a particular expression of male friendship common in Roman culture in which older men cultivated younger ones. These were unequal friendships and often included sexual expression, although they were not what we would recognise as 'permanent, faithful and stable' relationships.[2] Indeed, most of these older men were married. Scholars suggest that the words used in this passage refer to the passive recipients of anal intercourse (soft, effeminate, passive, lacking virility) and the pederasts who were condemned because they 'wasted their seed' and corrupted young men (infantilised and feminised them).

If the only expression of homosexuality familiar to Paul was pederasty or prostitution, it can easily been seen why this was problematic for him as it would be for us. (And think about the way in which this connection is still made between paedophiles and homosexuals, although most abuse is carried out by heterosexual men even when it involves both male and female children.) However, when we read the word 'homosexual' in these texts today, we are imposing onto Paul's writing a modern concept that belongs to our world, not to his. We are thinking about a different category of relationship, whereas Paul's ethical instructions are addressed to first-century men using first-century moral categories that reflect his own hybrid cultural identity as an observant Jew, with a Greek education, growing up in the Roman Empire.

There is no consensus over whether Paul could have known homosexual relationships which were not exploitative but which embodied a partnership of equals. Loveday Alexander says:

Paul might have known the 'Platonic' ideal from classical literature (though as a Jew he would have found it as abhorrent). But even if he did, it would not offer a model of faithful and stable same-sex relationships: such relationships...were inherently unequal, impermanent, and non-exclusive. In the Roman world (and especially in the mercantile/artisan urban circles in which Paul moved), same-sex relationships were most likely to be with rent-boys or with household slaves. In other words, Paul doesn't condemn long-term, faithful same-sex relationships, for the simple reason that he doesn't know them: the homosexual activity he knows falls under the category *porneia* ('bad sex') because it is either abusive (abuse within the family unit, including slave-rape) or commercially exploitative. Paul's disapproval of particular sexual practices actually protects the rights of the vulnerable within the Roman household. In Roman times, having a sexual relationship with a social inferior – male or female slaves, dependents or prostitutes – did not count as adultery: this was simply a normal expression of adult male power, especially within the household.[3]

What we might want to decide is whether Paul is simply condemning a particular form of behaviour or whether he is condemning a lifestyle. If we believe that Paul condemns homosexuality as a lifestyle it can be argued that he does so because he identifies it as a pagan phenomenon, as we will explore further in a moment.

To some extent, all of Paul's condemnation of particular sexual practices depends on a hierarchical distinction between gender roles. It is the identification of men with the female role in sexual relationships that is the main problem. This is the connection between this issue and the issues of gender distinctiveness which we looked at earlier. This perspective is reinforced by reading Romans 1:26–27 as a prohibition on men assuming the passive role in intercourse.

ROMANS 1:18–32

For the wrath of God is revealed from heaven against all ungodliness and wickedness of those who by their wickedness suppress the truth.

For what can be known about God is plain to them, because God has shown it to them.

Ever since the creation of the world his eternal power and divine nature, invisible though they are, have been understood and seen through the things he has made. So they are without excuse;

for though they knew God, they did not honour him as God or give thanks to him, but they became futile in their thinking, and their senseless minds were darkened.

Claiming to be wise, they became fools;

and they exchanged the glory of the immortal God for images resembling a mortal human being or birds or four-footed animals or reptiles.

Therefore God gave them up in the lusts of their hearts to impurity, to the degrading of their bodies among themselves, because they exchanged the truth about God for a lie and worshipped and served the creature rather than the Creator, who is blessed for ever! Amen.

For this reason God gave them up to degrading passions. Their women exchanged natural intercourse for unnatural,

and in the same way also the men, giving up natural intercourse with women, were consumed with passion for one another. Men committed shameless acts with men and received in their own persons the due penalty for their error.

And since they did not see fit to acknowledge God, God gave them up to a debased mind and to things that should not be done.

They were filled with every kind of wickedness, evil, covetousness, malice. Full of envy, murder, strife, deceit, craftiness, they are gossips,

slanderers, God-haters, insolent, haughty, boastful, inventors of evil, rebellious towards parents,

foolish, faithless, heartless, ruthless.

They know God's decree, that those who practise such things deserve to die – yet they not only do them but even applaud others who practise them.

Let's just walk through this passage so that we understand Paul's argument. He begins by explaining that God has revealed himself through his Creation, so that anyone, even pagans, ought to be able to know God. Instead, some have exchanged the proper worship of God for the worship of false gods, carved idols resembling animals and birds. As a result, God 'gave them up' and left them to do what they wanted, including unnatural sex, which because it is against God's law (and Paul would argue, natural law) will lead eventually to death without salvation.

Sexuality, which ought to be a blessing from God, has now become a curse. There is some dispute about the character of that curse, and in particular of the specific meaning of verses 26–28. While many scholars assume that the term 'unnatural intercourse' relates to homosexual and lesbian sex, others have suggested that it simply refers to anal intercourse (prohibited because of the command that sex should be procreative). Still others consider that it is the passionate nature of sex which Paul disapproves of – relating it to the kind of sex which took place in pagan worship and practice, including sex with prostitutes, both male and female. In particular, all passion, or extreme emotion, is dishonourable because it 'enslaves' a person – and in particular with relation to men, it subjugates them. Where women are driven to these passions, they are not only giving in to the 'flesh' but subverting the hierarchy, avoiding proper submission to men and in particular to their husbands.

In taking all these passages together, it would be hard to argue that the Bible does not have a problem with certain kinds of sexual activity, in particular anal intercourse between men. However, as we have seen, this prohibition is based on two very strong ideas: the first is that of a hierarchy between men and women which defines the right roles between them in sexual relationships, and the second is the importance of preserving semen for the procreation of children. As we have seen, some people will want to preserve these ideas across cultures, while others will consider that the world has changed so radically since these texts were written that we should not consider ourselves morally bound by the prohibition against non-procreative sexual activity, or same-sex desire.

Questions

- What tensions do you experience between biblical teaching and your conscience?
- What challenges can you see in those tensions?

Same-sex desire: science and sociology

As we saw earlier, one of the issues that arises in translating the letters of St Paul is the use of the term 'homosexual' as if it described a category of people, and not a specific activity. In fact, same-sex desire was not seen as marker of identity until the late 19th century, when the term 'homosexual' was coined by a Hungarian writer, Karl-Maria Benkert, in 1869 and subsequently taken up and disseminated much more widely by Richard von Krafft-Ebbing in his 1886 book *Psychopathia Sexualis*. The word 'homosexual' is a Greek and Latin hybrid, with the first element derived from Greek *homos*, 'same', connoting sexual acts and affections between members of the same sex. Benkert was convinced that homosexuality was an innate characteristic and not a choice for some men. This was the beginning of the movement towards identifying homosexuality as an issue of identity rather than a description of particular sexual activities. As we will see, this has an impact on the way that moral and ethical choices regarding sexual activity are understood.

This new language emerged around the time that Freud was defining psychosexual development in gendered terms, describing the way in which little boys and little girls grew up and grew to understand desire in relationship to their fathers and mothers. Homosexuality was seen as an aberrant developmental outcome and was deemed to be a psychiatric disorder for many years. Until 1973 homosexuality was classified as a mental illness in Britain. The Roman Catholic Church still considers that those who experience homosexual orientation are 'objectively disordered' because their orientation leads to a tendency to 'moral evil'.[4] While the current pope has taken a less judgemental view, he continues to stress the importance of the traditional family unit and to oppose equal marriage and adoption rights for same-sex couples.

It is possible that the adoption of more fluid approaches to both gender and sexuality will lead to a situation in which, once again, there are no categories of people associated with particular sexual acts, but that the acts themselves will be differentiated. However, we are some way from seeing how this will play out in the 21st century, and for the time being there is still a clear identification in most people's minds between identity and sexual desire.

SCIENCE AND SAME-SEX ATTRACTION

We've seen how both religion and early psychology considered same-sex attraction as a deviation. Attitudes have changed in the scientific world, and the question of whether sexual orientation is 'natural' or 'unnatural' has tended to be asked not so much by scientists but in the context of religious debates, with anti-homosexual advocates insisting that homosexuality is unnatural and their opponents insisting it is natural.

What can it mean to ask if homosexuality is natural? It has at least three different interpretations:

- First, does homosexuality occur in nonhuman animals?
- Second, is homosexuality a result of human evolution?
- Third, is homosexuality consistent with natural law?

The third question is philosophical rather than scientific and should be treated with extreme caution. By contrast, the first two interpretations of the question are scientifically meaningful and interesting, bearing in mind that answers to both are of no moral consequence.

One of the main issues in this debate concerns the degree to which sexual orientation manifests, and is recognised, in a similar manner across cultures, both geographically and historically. Those who believe that sexual orientation is socially constructed emphasise cultural variation, whereas those who believe that it is an essential human trait are impressed with its cross-cultural regularities. Many of the terms used in the nature/nurture debate are fraught with moral implications which they cannot bear. So, for example, people will use the terms 'biological', 'genetic', 'hereditary', 'heritable', 'innate', 'inborn', 'natural' and 'essential' as equivalent to 'natural', and the terms 'chosen', 'learned', 'environmental', 'socialised', 'unnatural' and 'socially constructed' as equivalent to 'acquired' or 'nurtured'. Some suggest that the use of these terms implies that it is possible to talk about the difference between what is essential and what is socially constructed, while everything else in between is imprecise and should be avoided.

If we take this view, we can quickly see that the whole area is fraught with culturally, socially or religiously defined terms which are not scientific in their character (although many would claim that they are).

The prevalence of same-sex attraction is also a source of debate, primarily because those for whom it is a problem want to suggest that it is rare, and thus a minority aberration from the norm, while those for whom it is not a problem want to suggest that it is common and thus 'natural'. The rates of occurrence are particularly difficult to ascertain. While on the one hand many countries now have equal rights for same-sex couples, including the right to marriage in 23 countries, on the other hand there are 75 countries that legally proscribe homosexual behaviour. Eleven countries – all in Africa, Asia and the Middle East – retain the death penalty as a possible sanction for homosexual acts. In these circumstances we are unlikely to be able to gather cross-cultural statistics about same-sex attraction.

Similarly, there have been recent attempts to review the literature which have demonstrated just how difficult it is to 'prove' someone's same-sex attraction. Although the phenomena of sexual orientation (behaviour, attraction, identity and arousal) tend to go together – homosexually oriented people tend to identify as gay or lesbian and to have sex with same-sex partners – they do not always. For example, some men who identify as straight/heterosexual have sex with other men and appear to be most strongly attracted to men.

Some adolescents engage in homosexual activity yet grow up to identify and behave as heterosexuals. Similarly, some individuals pursue same-sex relationships in sex-segregated environments, such as boarding schools, prisons or the armed services, but resume heterosexual relationships once other-sex partners are available.

The degree of association among homosexual attraction, behaviour and identity varies across individuals in different cultural contexts. For example, in some cultures and communities, homosexually attracted men regularly engage in same-sex behaviour while still maintaining a heterosexual identity. In other cultures and communities, such a pattern may be less common, and homosexually attracted men may find it difficult to find male partners without identifying themselves as homosexual or bisexual.

When Kinsey conducted the first large surveys of homosexuality in the United States during the 1940s, his results shocked readers because they made homosexual behaviour and attractions appear so common. In his surveys 37 per cent of men admitted having had a homosexual experience. Most of these occurred during adolescence, perhaps indicating brief experimentation. Approximately 10 per cent of the men had been more or less exclusively homosexual for at least three years during adulthood – this is the origin of the '10 per cent of people are homosexual' assertion that was commonly made until recent and more representative surveys supported lower rates. About 4 per cent of his male respondents had been homosexual for their entire lives.[5]

Asking about sexual identity – whether respondents consider themselves homosexual/gay/lesbian, bisexual, or heterosexual/straight – is perhaps the simplest way to survey people about sexual orientation. A national survey of sexual identity in 2016 indicated that 93 per cent of the population identified as heterosexual, 1 per cent as exclusively homosexual or lesbian, 2.8 per cent as lesbian gay or bisexual, and 4 per cent were unwilling to comment or did not know.[6]

Although the nature/nurture debate rages with regard to sexuality just as it does with regard to gender behaviour, there seems to be a correlation between beliefs about the causes of sexual orientation and degrees of tolerance of homosexuality based on the following logic: if there are biological causes that lead certain people to be homosexual, then those people were never entirely free to be heterosexual and hence cannot be held responsible for their homosexuality. For example, finding a gene that increases the chance a man will be homosexual would mean that the man is not completely free to choose to be heterosexual and we should neither blame him nor discriminate against him.

However, even if orientation is governed by genetics, that does not imply that someone who has such an orientation has no choice about their behaviour. It is wrong to suggest that simply because someone has a 'homosexual gene' they cannot make choices. Indeed, whether we have a genetic trait, or have been conditioned by our upbringing, we also have the capacity to make choices, as humans with free will. The significance comes in recognising that even if we cannot choose our feelings and desires, we can choose our behaviour.

Consider the following two sentences:

- 'I choose to have sex with partners of my own sex.'
- 'I choose to desire to have sex with partners of my own sex.'

The first sentence is conventional and sensible; the second sentence is neither. Applied to sexual orientation, it makes sense to say that people choose their sexual partners, but it doesn't make sense to say that they choose their desires.

Sexual orientation is defined as relative desire for same-sex or other-sex sex partners. Thus, it does not make sense to say that one chooses one's sexual orientation. And to take the argument one step further, if, as we have seen, desire exists on a spectrum, it does not make sense to say that one can choose to engage in activity which is inconsistent with one's sexual orientation, only that sexual orientation may be more or less consistent for some people.

The treatment of people who identify as homosexual has changed significantly in the past fifty years in Europe and the United States, as we saw in Chapter 1. One consequence of this has been that cultural expressions of homosexuality are much more prevalent and obvious. Perhaps as early as the late 19th century, one reaction to the negative labelling of homosexuality (by Freud for example) was to claim it as a positive identity and to flaunt particular cultural expressions, such as cross-dressing. Throughout the 20th century there were increasingly public displays of gender-transgressive culture, for example in cross-dressing music hall acts, camp comedians and drag artists. While no means all of the people engaged in these forms of entertainment were lesbian or gay, they provided a code which people could choose to adopt or not. The adoption of particular dress codes can be seen in the gay liberation 'Pride' marches of the 1980s where gay men and women chose to dress in ways which visibly identified them as belonging to a particular subculture. These included gay men dressing in biker leathers, tight-fitting sportswear or cowboy dress, and lesbians donning dungarees and Doc Martin boots.

In more recent years greater tolerance of gender fluidity has arguably diminished the impact of both gendered and transgressive cultural expressions, in both men and women's dress choices, employment and family roles. However, in some cultures the adoption of male dress by a woman may be seen as a signifier of lesbianism and not simply a fashion decision, while a man who participates in sex with a male prostitute may not identify as homosexual because he is married with children.

It could be argued that, as conspicuous prejudice has diminished, the need for such subcultures has also receded. As long ago as 2005 Andrew Sullivan, a prominent gay academic, described this in his local American context:

Go watch a gay rugby team compete in a regional tournament with straight teams and you will see how vast but subtle the revolution has been. And, in fact, this is the trend: gay civil associations in various ways are interacting with parallel straight associations in a way that leaves their gay identity more and more behind. They're rugby players first, gay rugby players second.[7]

However, as I pointed out earlier, this is by no means a universal experience. Even in the 'tolerant' Western world and despite improved legal rights, many LGBTQIA+ people experience prejudice and difficulty in living freely according to their self-understanding and desires. There is widespread agreement that the suicide rate among young LGBTQIA+ people is higher than that of the general population.[8]

Questions

- What stories do you know, or experiences do you have, of those who experience same-sex desire or would self-identify as gay or lesbian?
- What is your attitude to those people and how has it been shaped?

6
MARRIAGE

Marriage can be seen as both a social contract and a divine gift. Relationships which are long lasting enable individuals to grow in maturity, wisdom and self-knowledge as well as self-giving. They guarantee the care of the vulnerable, both children and the aged. Marriage ensures the proper care of children. But we could ask whether other relationships might provide the same stability and responsibility – for individual parents and the whole of society.

Marriage in the Bible

Marriage as a concept has been redefined throughout Judeo-Christian history; it is not a single unchanging idea that can be traced from Genesis to the present day. We can see this not only in the biblical record itself, but also in the practice of marriage and partnership through history. This is particularly true if we consider the contemporary expectation in the developed world that marriage is the culmination of romantic love, whereas for thousands of years it has been primarily an economic and political institution.

The character of marriage in the Old Testament is contested, but it is clearly the case that the patriarchs, Abraham, Israel, Joshua and the early kings of Israel practised polygamy. By the first century BCE, this practice seems to have died out among the Jews, and Jesus certainly expects that a man will have one wife. However, it can be argued that the model of marriage was patriarchal, or at least patricentric – that is, focused on the male line, through ancestry; located in the male household, as women moved from the home of their birth family to that of their husbands on marriage; and patriarchal in so far as the father was the head of the household. Feminists have argued that patriarchy is an unmitigated 'bad thing' but some theologians would argue that like all forms of social organisation it is distorted by human sin. Patriarchy, they contest, provides stability and protection to families.[1]

On the other hand, arguably both Jesus and Paul prioritised celibacy over marriage. For Jesus himself to reach the age of thirty without being married would have been extremely unusual in the culture of his day, when it was the responsibility of men and women to marry and bring children into the world – participating in God's work of Creation. There are two examples of Jesus teaching about marriage, and one of these takes the form of a conflict about divorce. Jesus begins from the accepted Jewish teaching, but takes a more radical position, going further than his Jewish contemporaries. Rabbi Shammai taught that a man could divorce his wife only for adultery. Rabbi Hillel on the other hand taught that a man could divorce his wife for many reasons. And later, Rabbi Akiva famously taught that a man could divorce his wife for any reason, 'even if he find one fairer than she'. But, as we shall see, Jesus takes a more nuanced view.

MATTHEW 19:3–12

Some Pharisees came to him and to test him they asked, 'Is it lawful for a man to divorce his wife for any cause?'

He answered, 'Have you not read that he who made them from the beginning "made them male and female,"

and said, "For this reason a man shall leave his father and mother and be joined to his wife, and the two shall become one flesh"?

So they are no longer two but one flesh. What therefore God has joined together, let not man put asunder.'

They said to him, 'Why then did Moses command us to give a certificate of dismissal and to divorce her?'

He said to them, 'It was because you were so hard-hearted that Moses allowed you to divorce your wives, but at the beginning it was not so.

And I say to you, whoever divorces his wife, except for unchastity, and marries another commits adultery.'

His disciples said to him, 'If such is the case of a man with his wife, it is better not to marry.'

But he said to them, 'Not everyone can accept this teaching, but only those to whom it is given.

For there are eunuchs who have been so from birth, and there are eunuchs who have been made eunuchs by others, and there are eunuchs who have made themselves eunuchs for the sake of the kingdom of heaven. Let anyone accept this who can.'

Many scholars have argued that the most significant aspect of Jesus' teaching is not the prohibition on divorce, but the greater responsibility given to the husband to observe the permanence of marriage. Jesus' teaching protects the more vulnerable partner, the woman in this instance, who has no means of providing for herself outside marriage or dependence on her father or brothers.

Many have argued that Jesus makes a pastoral accommodation for the failure of marriage, even if the ideal is lifelong faithfulness.

Elsewhere (Luke 20:34–36), when presented with a problem about a woman with more than one husband, and asked to which man she will be married in heaven, Jesus deflects the question by stating that there will be no marriage in heaven, since our resurrection bodies will have no need of marriage. We will come back to this idea in the final chapter.

The issue of marriage is of more concern to St Paul and clearly troubled many in the early church. They were worried about intermarriage between pagans and Christians, as well as the place of marriage in the Christian life. These anxieties were clearly influenced by the expectation of the imminent second coming and a sense that all human relationships are transitory. For this reason, St Paul counsels people to remain either in their single or their married state. Marriage should be the last resort of the desperate, as a remedy against sin – that is, sexual immorality.

But it can also be argued that Paul has a universally poor view of sexual desire and he certainly never refers to its value in the procreation of children. He seems to have been a single man, and for him celibacy is the ideal and marriage is a poor second best, although he admits, 'It is better to marry than burn' (1 Corinthians 7:9) – the New Revised Standard Version translates burn as 'to be inflamed with passion'.

We find more teaching in the letters known as the 'pastoral epistles' which emerged from the growing church. Whereas the first Christian communities were radically different in their social makeup from the communities in which they were set – for example, women were able to lead, teach and pray in public – as the church grew it gained an institutional status which reflected Roman culture, both the Roman civic culture and Roman household culture, and the role of women became more restricted.

The pastoral letters reflect a hierarchical set-up, in which men oversee the household just as the 'presbyters' (overseers) were taking authority over the church. This same approach is taken to old and young, women and slaves: both in terms of obedience, but also in the care and responsibility expected towards the 'weaker' or 'junior' members of the household. However, they differ in one important respect and that is in the expectations on husbands.

EPHESIANS 5:25–33

Husbands, love your wives, just as Christ loved the church and gave himself up for her, in order to make her holy by cleansing her with the washing of water by the word,

so as to present the church to himself in splendour, without a spot or wrinkle or anything of the kind – yes, so that she may be holy and without blemish.

In the same way, husbands should love their wives as they do their own bodies. He who loves his wife loves himself.

For no one ever hates his own body, but he nourishes and tenderly cares for it, just as Christ does for the church,

because we are members of his body.

'For this reason a man will leave his father and mother and be joined to his wife, and the two will become one flesh.'

This is a great mystery, and I am applying it to Christ and the church.

Each of you, however, should love his wife as himself, and a wife should respect her husband.

The writer of Ephesians exhorts husbands to 'love your wife as Christ loved the church and gave himself up for it'. First, what is being described here, in contrast to the prevailing power dynamics, is a relationship of self-sacrifice in which the more powerful individual puts the interests of the weaker first. Second, if we understand the church to be the community given birth by the Holy Spirit at Pentecost, then Christ's death released the potential for the church to fully become itself (or, note the metaphor, 'herself'), just as marriage should release a woman to become most fully herself.

Where interpretations of this passage of Scripture vary will return us to questions of gender and whether or not a woman is most fully herself in a complementary role to that of her husband.

Marriage in tradition: the church

As we have seen, one of the ways in which the church has tried to understand the purpose of any human activity in matters of ethics is to ask what the end/*telos*/goal of the activity is intended to be by God. Historically, as we have seen, the primary *telos* of sexual activity has been identified as the procreation of children. If this is accepted then the need for intercourse to take place within a stable relationship in which children can be nurtured and protected makes sense. This is why Thomas Aquinas, for example, thought that sexual intercourse outside marriage was a sin, because it led to the possibility of a child being born without the care and protection of a mother and father.

The church recognises marriage as both a social institution and a gift from God. It is therefore available to everyone, regardless of faith, but given a special quality of grace when blessed by the church. As we will see, for much of history the role of the church was simply to act as a guarantor that a marriage, understood as a contract between two individuals entered into freely, had taken place.

The Church of England tends to articulate its theology of marriage, through in its liturgy and canon law rather than its teaching documents. The 1662 Book of Common Prayer speaks of marriage as:

> an honourable estate, instituted of God in the time of man's innocency, signifying unto us the mystical union that is betwixt Christ and his Church; which holy estate Christ adorned and beautified with his presence, and first miracle that he wrought, in Cana of Galilee; and is commended of Saint Paul to be honourable among all men: and therefore is not by any to be enterprised, nor taken in hand, unadvisedly, lightly, or wantonly, to satisfy men's carnal lusts and appetites, like brute beasts that have no understanding; but reverently, discreetly, advisedly, soberly, and in the fear of God; duly considering the causes for which Matrimony was ordained.

In the Book of Common Prayer, the purposes of marriage are given as:

- the procreation of children
- a remedy against sin
- and for the mutual society, help and comfort of the partners.

It was notable in the revised marriage service in the *Alternative Service Book* (ASB) and now in Common Worship that these good things are put in reverse order, so that marriage is a gift through which the partners grow in grace as they:

- grow in love and trust
- enjoy sexual union
- nurture children.

The church makes an appeal to tradition in stating that marriage is a social good and the family is an institution which benefits those within it and especially children. The redefining of marriage to emphasise companionship over parenthood, not only in the church, but in society at large, places the value of the institution as one in which both adults flourish. This has to be seen alongside the historical experience of marriage which was frequently an instrument of patriarchy which denied women access to property or status apart from that derived from their husbands.

For much of human history marriage has been first and foremost a privilege of the wealthy, and a tool of diplomacy or financial gain. For ordinary people these were domestic arrangements; marriage rites were by nature in this time domestic rites with religious implications. Home and hearth, kin and community were aspects of life so fundamental that they were intricately related to human spirituality but not so centrally focused on explicitly religious liturgical acts.

While there is some evidence that, in the very early church, Christian couples might have married in rites held within the faith community, there is no evidence to suggest this was common practice across the diverse geography of the early church world or in the first generation of the Christian church. In this period betrothal was seen as essential to a proper marriage and formed a basic contract of commitment between two households. This required the consent to the relationship given by the groom and the agent who gave the bride, usually her father. Marriage blessings were usually domestic in nature and often took place at feasts, on the household threshold, or at the marriage bed.

As the church of the late medieval period was restricting its understanding of how Christians were to understand sacrament, marriage came to be seen as one of the seven sacraments of the church. Both the man and the woman were now seen as entering into a sacramental act, and now both the man and woman were expected to voice their consent. Vows were exchanged: vows that in most circumstances (but not all) required the woman to swear her obedience to her husband.

A life-transforming process that had formerly been left in the hands of families and communities who sought God's blessing on it was now authoritatively placed in the hands of the official, priest-led church, with clearly structured expectations and obligations prescribed and demanded by the church and the assurance of clear, spiritual benefit to be derived from formal marriage with its sacramental nuptial blessing. Theologians of the 12th and 13th centuries considered marriage to be a sacrament (a teaching codified in the 1563 Council of Trent). If marriage is a sacrament, then it makes something happen and leads to an objective or ontological change which cannot be undone. Thus the Catholic doctrine of the indissolubility of marriage was formulated. This created problems with regard to failed and childless marriages, particularly among royalty and aristocracy, and led almost immediately to the possibility of declaring a marriage null (that is, no marriage at all).

Although it is a caricature to suggest that the break between the

Roman Catholic Church and the Church of England was caused by the failure of the pope to grant Henry VIII an annulment of his marriage to Catherine of Aragon, it is not usually remembered that this marriage was indeed annulled – as the concept of divorce, in which the legitimacy of children was retained after the dissolution of a marriage – did not really exist. As the Church of England began to formulate its own doctrines, it dispensed with the teaching that marriage is a sacrament, although some Anglicans would still understand it in these terms.

A decisive break with the traditions of the medieval church was the permission given to priests and bishops to marry. Marriage, rather than celibacy, became the ideal state. The Protestant reformers saw marriage as an important source of companionship for the clergy, and stressed the importance of the family (rather than the church) as the place where faith would be nurtured.

The Book of Common Prayer assumes that betrothal takes place before marriage, and it is widely believed by historians that betrothal, rather than marriage, was the gateway to sexual activity. Until the 17th century the legal requirements for marriage in England were governed by canon law, i.e. church law. This covered issues such as the reading of banns or the issue of a license, and the places where a marriage might take place. However, none of these were mandatory and the absence of banns or a license – or even the fact that the marriage was not celebrated in a church – did not render the marriage void. The only indispensable requirement was that the marriage be celebrated by an Anglican clergyman.

In 1653, during the Puritan period of the English Commonwealth, the nature of marriage was once again reshaped by theological constraints. In this radical, Puritan setting, marriage became a simple vow between a man and a woman using a prescribed Puritan form from the *Directory for Public Worship*.[2] The vow was made before a justice of the peace, and there were no prayers and no ordained minister involved, making it absolutely clear that marriage was not to be understood as a sacramental act, thereby allowing considerably more latitude in arguing for the potential dissolubility of a marriage. Puritans saw marriage as an event with significant spiritual and religious implications, but this form of marriage ceremony, carried out in a manner that was totally divorced from church life, opened the way for a view of marriage as a legal, social and cultural event rather than a religious one.

Until the 18th century the assumption was that if a couple lived together and had children they were married, regardless of whether or not they had contracted the marriage legally or participated in a religious ceremony. This created so many problems, especially with the proliferation of non-Anglican religious sects who preferred not to have a ceremony in church, that the government was forced to act and in 1753 passed the Marriage Act in England requiring all marriages to be registered, wherever they took place, by a civil registrar. This took control of marriage out of the hands of the church, a move which would be consolidated by the introduction of civil marriage in 1837.

Marriage thus became, in law, a civil contract which could be either overlaid by religious meaning (including, for example, in the lives of people of other faiths) or free from religious meaning. Gradually fewer and fewer marriages were conducted in the Church of England, from 90 per cent in 1845 to 34 per cent in 1986 to 20 per cent in 2013. From 1837 onwards, the Church of England had to play its part in shaping the understanding of marriage in England through the presence of bishops in the House of Lords and the influence of its teaching on those in public life.

DIVORCE AND COHABITATION

We can see how both church and state thought about marriage in the changes to the law which followed, in particular with regard to divorce. Initially, the biblical prohibition on divorce was reflected in the civil law, except in the case of the extremely wealthy, where a man could be granted a divorce by an Act of Parliament. By gaining a divorce, the husband could seize all the property of a marriage, including that which had been inherited by the wife. Legislation passed in 1857 gave married women access to their own property and both men and women access to divorce in limited circumstances.

Changes in the law reflect a changed understanding of the relationship between sex and marriage. Whereas until the 19th century, only adultery was deemed to be a valid cause for divorce, and the lack of consummation, or consanguinity (too close a family relationship) a valid reason to dissolve a marriage, in recent years the reasons for ending marriages are more concerned with the quality of the relationship than with sexual conduct. In 1969 divorce law was extended to allow couples to divorce after they had been separated for two years. A marriage could be ended if it had irretrievably broken down, and neither partner had to prove 'fault' any longer. The period of time before a divorce could be sought was reduced to a year in 1984.

The longstanding link between marriage, sex and procreation was abolished with the church's acceptance of birth control for married people in the 1930s. However, the availability of birth control to all, regardless of their marriage state, legalised within the National Health Service in 1968, created a moral challenge for the church. As it became not only possible, but increasingly common, for people to have sexual relationships outside marriage that did not result in the birth of illegitimate children, the church found itself considering the problem of cohabitation in British society. Pastoral theology written at the time generally assumes that this is a reality, but varies in its response.

In Britain today the average age for first sexual intercourse is 16. In 2013 the average age for a first marriage was 30.6 years for women and 32.5 for men. Clearly, for the vast majority of people in Britain the link between sexual activity and marriage has been broken.

Indeed, it seems as if the link between marriage and having children has also been substantially broken. Where once cohabitation might have been seen as a preliminary to marriage (a trial period, which might last a few years), increasingly, marriage is seen as the culmination or sealing of a relationship, taking place, if at all, after children have been born. The idea of 'common law marriage' still persists in the public mind, even though no such concept exists in law. In 2016 the percentage of children born outside marriage or civil partnerships was 48 per cent, of whom only a third were born to single parents (in the mid-1950s less than 5 per cent of children were born to unmarried mothers).[3]

So how does the church respond to this practical and pastoral reality? The latest guidance was issued by the House of Bishops in 1999 and is still on the Church of England website. It clearly offers an open door to couples wishing to explore marriage while already living together, and there is no indication that any kind of repentance for their previous relationship outside marriage would be expected. The Church of England wedding site goes even further, noting that 'One in five couples who come to church for a wedding already has children.'[4] The site goes on to reassure couples that children can be involved in the ceremony, and even suggests that baptism could take place during the same service.

Marriage in the tradition: theology

Some Christians who are supportive of permanent, faithful, stable same-sex partnerships may not agree that these should be understood as the same thing as marriage. They may take this view from the perspective of Scripture or tradition, feeling that marriage has particular characteristics which cannot be expressed in a same-sex relationship. This is a matter of personal conscience, although lay people have a freedom to act here in a way which the clergy do not, as marriage is not open to clergy in a partnership with someone of the same gender at present.

Some people will emphasise the nature of friendship in both

marriage and same-sex partnerships as being more significant than the sexual relationship or the nurture of children. Some theologians have argued that neither the sacramental nor covenantal understandings of marriage are dependent on the link between sex and procreation, and that a definition of marriage which assumes this close link is at fault.

Definitions of marriage which see procreation as a necessary condition of its purpose not only deny the sacrament of marriage to those with, for example, a disability or an intersex condition, but are no longer fully supported by the Church of England since it has allowed the use of contraception in marriage and made no distinction with regard to the status of children conceived through methods such as IVF.

It is difficult to argue that the experience of a child born through IVF, adopted as a baby by infertile parents, or otherwise welcomed into and nurtured by a family is of less value to God than the experience of a child who is the result of a sexual union between its parents. All such relationships are opportunities for God's grace and love to be at work.

MARRIAGE AS SACRAMENT

The Church of England does not teach that marriage is a sacrament, but many within the church would understand marriage in these terms. What is notable is that there is agreement that the church does not marry the couple, but rather blesses something that the couple themselves have done. The effective action in marriage is the exchange of vows and rings ('with this ring I thee wed') carried out by the couple; they are the ministers of the sacrament to each other.

Sacraments are occasions of grace in which we participate in the life of God. Just as we know that God is in relationship with God, through the indwelling of the Trinity, so we can understand human relationships, particularly as they are experienced in mutual sexual self-giving, as deriving from and participating in the relational character of God.

This can be particularly seen in the metaphors that are used to describe the relationship between Christ and the church. When the church is described as the bride of Christ, it is the character of self-giving, or self-sacrifice, which is being evoked. Just as Christ gave himself for the life of the church, so the participants in marriage give themselves, their bodies and their lives, to one another in mutual love.

For Rowan Williams, it is the combination of fidelity, commitment, and mutuality that open up the possibility for a sexual relationship to be sacramental:

> To be formed in our humanity by the loving delight of another is an experience whose contours we can identify most clearly and hopefully if we have also learned or are learning about being the object of the causeless loving delight of God, being the object of God's love for God through incorporation into the community of God's Spirit and the taking-on of the identity of God's child.[5]

But it is also important to recognise that intimacy between two people goes beyond sexual intimacy. By taking the time to really get to know another person, we give ourselves to them, to listen, to empathise, to support and encourage them – to sacrifice our needs to theirs.

MARRIAGE AS COVENANT

In marriage two individuals come together and promise that they will be faithful to each other (this may include sexual fidelity and emotional loyalty), that the relationship has the intention to be lifelong and life giving. These promises have the nature of a covenant, in that they are deemed to go beyond a legal contract, and to have a character which both imitates and participates in God's relationship with God's people, as exemplified in the biblical covenants with Noah, Abraham and Moses and the new covenant of salvation in Jesus.

Whether marriage is a sacrament or a covenant, it is a promise made between two people and Christians will take such promises, made before God, extremely seriously. They would share with anthropologists like Arnold van Gennep and Victor Turner the belief that marriage creates a new status and new state of life for the partners. This is expressed not only in sexual fidelity, but also in social standing and the place in the wider family. Breaking such a promise has implications not simply for the individual but for the family and for wider society.

MARRIAGE AND REASON: FRIENDSHIP

Aristotle considers friendship a virtue – that is, something which helps people to live good lives. He suggests there are three main reasons why one person might like someone else. One might like someone because they are good, or useful, or pleasant. When two individuals recognise that the other person is someone of good character, and they spend time with each other, engaged in activities that exercise their virtues, then they form one kind of friendship. Aristotle says that virtuous friendship depends on equality. When two people are equally virtuous, their friendship is perfect. If, however, there is a large gap in their moral development (as between a parent and a small child, or – Aristotle says – between a husband and a wife), then although their relationship may be based on the other person's good character, it will be imperfect precisely because of their inequality.

Aristotle cannot quite decide whether friendship depends on reciprocity and is instrumental – we engage in it for mutual benefit, or non-instrumental – we engage in it for its own sake. His three categories are contradictory in this respect (to like someone for being good is non-instrumental, but to like them because they are useful is instrumental). It is striking that in his *Ethics* Aristotle never thinks of saying that the uniting factor in all friendships is the desire each friend has for the good of the other.

Later philosophers and ethicists, beginning with Kant, and

including Sam Wells in our own time, would argue that true friendship cannot be instrumental: we must enjoy our friends for their own sake, not ours.

Anselm of Canterbury took the basic idea of the virtue of friendship and gave it Christian character by considering not only the themes of reciprocity and equality, but also friendship with the saints, who give us access to God in a kind of three-way relationship (because they are 'friends of God'). Anselm sees a friend as someone to whom he is bound and from whom he can learn as together they turn towards God in prayer and worship.

Friendship was a particular virtue of monastic life which was, in itself, a way in which men and women could absent themselves from the responsibilities of family, within the assumption of celibacy. Friendship could be seen as a mutual gazing towards Christ, for example in the lives of Clare and Francis, John of the Cross and Theresa of Avila, and Aelred of Rievaulx and his monastic brothers. Within celibate communities one could love another as oneself, but that person would be one to whom one has no responsibilities of family or commitment, so this could be considered a relationship of equals. At least in classical and medieval times in Europe, and probably until the 18th century, it was inconceivable that there could be virtuous friendship between men and women in secular life because of the difference in their status.

Perhaps this is one reason for the contrast between friendship and love found in popular understanding, especially love understood as sexually expressed. In our time, the idea of friendship has, arguably, been debased by the over-sexualisation of society (and the influence of Freud) which struggles to see any relationship as asexual. However, friendship, as we have seen, has now become an expectation of the relationship within marriage. In the developed West, at least, marriages are seen as relationships of equals in which virtuous friendship is not only possible but desirable, and in Christian marriage, friendship can also be seen as the mutual gaze on God.

There has been some acceptance of committed same-sex friendship within the Church of England, but such friendships, particularly among the clergy, are expected to be celibate, that is, to exclude sexual relationships. This was the outcome of the church's debates over civil partnership. The debate demonstrated that the church is conflicted over the moral status of same-sex relationships and, indeed, the moral status of the clergy. By teaching that the clergy should order their lives to a higher moral standard than lay people, allowing only celibate civil partnerships and subsequently denying the clergy equal marriage, the church says that same-sex relationships fall short of God's ideal, but allows them as a form of 'pastoral accommodation'.

While friendship is important, it is given a richness through the sexual dimension, and we ought not to suppress the importance of sex in binding friendships together in covenanted relationships (as any married person knows, sex can be a source of comfort and an expression of forgiveness, as well as mutual pleasure or fun).

It may be helpful in thinking about the place of sexual desire to remember that it is not the only form of desire which shapes our relationships. Desire can be for wisdom or virtue and our admiration or desire for another person can be driven by their wisdom or virtue as much as by their physical attributes, just as lust or eros can also be aroused by money, achievement and power!

Questions

- What do you think the relationship between marriage and the procreation of children should be?
- Is marriage the right category of relationship for people in same-sex relationships?

7
LOOKING FORWARD

As I hope you have been reminded in reading this book, we humans are complicated beings, shaped by our biology, nurture, society and beliefs. We often think of identity (and thus faith, gender and sexuality) as things that belong to us as individuals shaped by our singular experience, but in fact we cannot make sense of who we are except through the feedback we get from our relationships with others. As we develop, formed by our experiences and that feedback, we start to tell a narrative, a story which connects those experiences through time. Our stories are both a way of confirming that in some way these things all happened to the same person, and evidence that we are capable of change.

The changes and challenges we face are often the motivation to seek a better or happier life, or greater satisfaction with the way we behave towards others. Whether we seek wisdom through experience, philosophy or religion, that search for happiness includes both the need to feel that we are acting with integrity – truth to ourselves – and charity – love for others. For Christians, being true to oneself will include being true to our baptismal incorporation into the body of Christ. Before a Christian is in relationship to anyone else, they are in relationship to God and this creates a deep sense of obligation to the rest of humankind also created to be in relationship to God.

One of the problems of contemporary Western culture is the repeated message that 'You can be anything you want to be' or 'You can live the dream'. While we might strive for success or happiness we must also accept our limitations, even before we struggle with the injustices and inequalities of our society. Actually, being willing to fail and learn from our failure is vital to learning any skill, whether driving, cooking or singing. And it is noticeable that all these examples require us to be willing to experiment with another person present, to develop relationships of trust in order to gain competence.

So, with these key themes in mind, let's revisit some of the topics covered in this book and consider both the potential and the limitations of our understanding and living out of gender and sexual relationships.

The issue of gender is currently fraught in the Western world by a new awareness of the power relationship between men and women and the way in which that can be exploited. It is notable that many of the high-profile examples relate to spheres in which expectations of men and women are radically different, contexts in which men are rewarded for their energy, power and dynamism while women are rewarded for their appearance, grooming and emotional intelligence or performance.

At the same time, many younger people are critiquing gender stereotyping to experiment with more fluid dress, makeup and behaviour. It would be easy to overstress the impact of high-profile performers and models, such as Tilda Swinton, Eddie Izard, Jack Monroe and others. Particularly in the fashion industry, the trend for androgynous models may disappear as quickly as it came. However, it is possible that what we are seeing is a more profound change in our understanding of gender and gender roles.

In considering how important gender identity seems to have become, it may be helpful to consider another concept that has become considerably more fluid in recent understanding – that of 'race'. It was once thought that to be 'black' was an enduring characteristic that existed across time, geography and culture. Not only that, but blackness was a characteristic given by God to differentiate people into roles and power relationships.

We can see now that it was a category defined in much of history by 'whiteness' and in particular by the 'whiteness' of colonising Europeans travelling across the globe encountering people of incredibly diverse skin colour, facial features and cultures. In the 18th century, it was the anti-slavery movement that first drew attention to the commonality between the slave owners and the slaves, in a sharp slogan, 'Am I not a man?' Not only did people have to be educated to see the 'black man' as an individual, but to differentiate between 'black' men to see them as diverse in their identities and stories.

This example may help to highlight a couple of things. First, identity is at least partly culturally constructed, even if there are also innate biological differences between humans. Second, cultural construction relies on differences between individuals being considered important. Once, people believed that God had ordered the world into black and white people, just as God ordered the world into male and female, healthy and sick, rich and poor. Most Christians today would balk at the idea that God had ordered a world in which there must be rich and poor, who know their station and accept it. On the other hand, if we accelerate to a point where we believe that we are race blind or gender blind too quickly we may miss much of the residual bias which exists in society against those who were once (and may still be) seen as 'other'.

We are used to the idea that gender is a 'thing' that can be labelled and is in some way important. It is possible that people will still think that in a hundred years' time. But we should be open to the possibility that this will not be the case. Similarly, until very recently it has been assumed that sexual orientation is a 'thing' that can be described in binary terms. Kinsey's research showed that to be a simplistic understanding of human sexual experience, and a cursory viewing of the history of same-sex attraction demonstrates something similar. We think that sexual orientation is important, but in the future this may not be the case.

As we have seen, we cannot conflate gender identity with sexuality, as both exist on a spectrum (although, as we have also seen, the percentage of those experiencing either their gender or their sexuality as different from the cisgender, heterosexual norm, is fairly small). Contemporary society's fixation with gender and sexuality tends to focus the discussion of sexual desire into a purely physical realm and to ignore all other personal and social dimensions.

Humans need more than sex for happiness, and this is why sex has historically, culturally and religiously, been placed in the context of secure, permanent relationships which provide for other human needs such as companionship, security and physical survival. Relationships are not just about what we do with each other in bed, but what we do in the kitchen, the garden, on holiday and in rearing children. They are about our dreams and intentions, our care for our parents, our contribution to society. And as long as those relationships were expected to provide children, then they were also intended to provide a secure context for their nurture and protection. Although marriage has a chequered history, it still provides not only a legal and financial framework for such relationships, but also a moment of transition and celebration which many couples still choose. One sign of the significance of a wedding is the average cost, which some sources in Britain suggest may be as high as £27,000, the equivalent of a year's salary.[1]

As we have noted, marriage or an equivalent social or legal partnership, often undertaken after the birth of children, is now usually considered the crown of the relationship or the last symbol of permanence for the couple involved. It might well be argued that the recent focus in the church on the place of marriage is taking place in a context in which theologies and ethics of desire are by no means resolved. The church has failed, in most contexts, to convince people of the value of chastity, and has had very little to say about the conditions for good sexual relationships except within marriage. We might want to think seriously about the place of power or coercion, and the importance of trust, in situations in which two people make themselves physically available and thus extremely vulnerable to one another.

Some Christians will argue that we have clear guidance to help us to get gender and sex right. They will find evidence for the importance of male and female gender as necessarily complementary to one another in the Bible and will be clear that the teaching of the church should maintain that the only place for a sexual relationship is within the marriage of a man and a woman. Being willing and able to live within God's plan is evidence of our dependency on God and our faithfulness to him. They would argue that the pressure for change comes from those who are living self-centred, not God-centred, lives. They look at people striving for happiness through individual self-realisation; the trend towards identity as the marker of authenticity; the recall to rational or intellectual truth, and feel that all these are features of a world in which humans have raised themselves above God. Reading Romans 12:1–2, they argue that God has made it clear what is good, acceptable and perfect and that being able to live by God's law is evidence of faith and dependence on his will.

> I appeal to you therefore, brothers and sisters, by the mercies of God, to present your bodies as a living sacrifice, holy and acceptable to God, which is your spiritual worship.

> Do not be conformed to this world, but be transformed by the renewing of your minds, so that you may discern what is the will of God – what is good and acceptable and perfect.

Where people are unable to do this, whether because of their understanding of their gender or sexuality, these people would argue that this is a sign of disorder (that is, sin or illness) or disobedience.

Others might take a more fluid view. Rowan Williams in his recent book, *Being Human*, concludes that our lives are not something we can get right or a problem to be solved, but a project which we will each undertake in our own way.[2] While some ways are better than others, there is no one right way, except that of Jesus – understood primarily as the way of unity with God. We could argue that the conclusion is the same, that the fullness of humanity is dependence on God, but Dr Williams counsels care in being able to distinguish between true dependence and social control dressed up in religious language which is fraught with repression, dehumanisation and infantilisation.

There is some evidence in the Bible for Williams' more fluid approach, in particular when it comes to the issues of both gender and marriage. We can explore this through the rather unlikely topic of heaven. When Christians think about heaven they are thinking about the condition of being united with God in eternity, both individually and collectively. Thinking back to Augustine and Aquinas, this unity is the ultimate *telos* of human life and so is a good clue to what really matters in life before we reach its end.

I CORINTHIANS 15:35–49

But someone will ask, 'How are the dead raised? With what kind of body do they come?'

Fool! What you sow does not come to life unless it dies.

And as for what you sow, you do not sow the body that is to be, but a bare seed, perhaps of wheat or of some other grain.

But God gives it a body as he has chosen, and to each kind of seed its own body.

Not all flesh is alike, but there is one flesh for human beings, another for animals, another for birds, and another for fish.

There are both heavenly bodies and earthly bodies, but the glory of the heavenly is one thing, and that of the earthly is another.

There is one glory of the sun, and another glory of the moon, and another glory of the stars; indeed, star differs from star in glory.

So it is with the resurrection of the dead. What is sown is perishable, what is raised is imperishable.

It is sown in dishonour, it is raised in glory. It is sown in weakness, it is raised in power.

It is sown a physical body, it is raised a spiritual body. If there is a physical body, there is also a spiritual body.

Thus it is written, 'The first man, Adam, became a living being'; the last Adam became a life-giving spirit.

But it is not the spiritual that is first, but the physical, and then the spiritual.

The first man was from the earth, a man of dust; the second man is from heaven.

As was the man of dust, so are those who are of the dust; and as is the man of heaven, so are those who are of heaven.

Just as we have borne the image of the man of dust, we will also bear the image of the man of heaven.

This is a complex passage and I don't intend to cover all its complexity in detail. I do want to notice a couple of important points. First, while we will have bodies in heaven we cannot possibly imagine what they will be like. It would be like trying to imagine a tree from looking at an acorn, or a plant from looking at a grain of wheat.

But the second is that there will be some kind of continuity. The earthly bodies that we know now are united with spiritual bodies. We can know something of our final image in this lifetime just as we will take something of our earthly image with us in the next. What is not clear is what we will take with us. You might have seen criticism on social media of a cartoon image that circulated after Stephen Hawking's death, showing him standing amidst the stars, having left his wheelchair behind.[3] Disability activists were angry at the idea that Hawking would only be his true self when he regained his mobility (and presumably speech). The key question is whether our resurrection bodies will retain their disability, their gender, their sexuality?

We can read Galatians 3:28 ('In Christ there is no Greek or Jew...') as meaning that difference between individual humans has no purpose in the body of Christ, or we can read it to mean that in heaven we will be indifferent to that difference. For some the first interpretation is the most straightforward but it is not then clear whether we might maintain any differences and if so, which ones, while for others adherence to the latter interpretation is crucial, since it preserves the value of difference, for example in gender complementarity, while dispensing with anything, such as power imbalance, which devalues the individual. In human experience it is almost impossible to imagine preserving difference while experiencing it as entirely blessing, but perhaps it is not impossible to experience within the love of God? We can only imagine that there will be continuity and discontinuity: that somehow we will know ourselves and yet be transformed. Perhaps gender, like race, will no longer be something which concerns us in this new creation.

If we become like the angels, we will no longer be gendered and there will no longer be any need for sexual relationships. This is one interpretation of the outcome of a short encounter between Jesus and some Saducees who ambush him with a thorny problem.

MARK 12:18–25

Some Sadducees, who say there is no resurrection, came to him and asked him a question, saying,

'Teacher, Moses wrote for us that if a man's brother dies, leaving a wife but no child, the man shall marry the widow and raise up children for his brother.

There were seven brothers; the first married and, when he died, left no children;

and the second married her and died, leaving no children; and the third likewise;

none of the seven left children. Last of all the woman herself died.

In the resurrection whose wife will she be? For the seven had married her.'

Jesus said to them, 'Is not this the reason you are wrong, that you know neither the scriptures nor the power of God?

For when they rise from the dead, they neither marry nor are given in marriage, but are like angels in heaven.'

James Alison in *Raising Abel* reads the story of the Saducees' question about marriage as evidence of their foolishness: they do not understand that marriage is only necessary to maintain life and creation in the old order; in the new order – the general resurrection – life will be eternal and therefore procreation will not be necessary to preserve human existence.[4] For Alison this is proof that gender difference will no longer be necessary in heaven.

An interesting and different stance is taken by Ian Paul, who notes in particular both the relationship to the question of disability, and the reality of Jesus' risen body, bearing the scars of crucifixion, and offers this quotation from C.S. Lewis in defence of the idea that we will maintain our gender in heaven, although we may not experience it in the same way as we do now.

I think our present outlook might be like that of a small boy who, on being told that the sexual act was the highest bodily pleasure, should immediately ask whether you ate chocolates at the same time. On receiving the answer 'No', he might regard absence of chocolates as the chief characteristic of sexuality. In vain would you tell him that the reason why lovers in their carnal raptures don't bother about chocolates is that they have something better to think of. The boy knows chocolate: he does not know the positive thing that excludes it. We are in the same position. We know the sexual life; we do not know, except in glimpses, the other thing which, in Heaven, will leave no room for it.[5]

While I do not want, in any way, to deny the reality of the life we experience, and in particular the way in which we both act and suffer in relationship to one another both on a small scale and as participants in the global community, there is an underlying message in Christianity (and indeed in other religions, notably Buddhism) that says, 'There is more to life than this.' There are aspects of identity which will remain a mystery to us in this life at least. There are ethical decisions we will make, without any possibility of certainty that we are right.

The 17th-century philosopher Blaise Pascal described all human decisions as a wager, where our actions have significant consequences, but our ability to understand those consequences is flawed, particularly in the anticipation. While we can discern a great deal through reason, we are ultimately forced to gamble. Many Christians understand the ethical decisions we make in faith in a similar way: we choose to take a gamble on the truth of the Bible, on the value of tradition, or on our own consciences. I hope that this book has provided you with an insight into some of the many resources which inform the decisions that others make, and might enable you to articulate the decisions you have made with greater insight.

WHAT THE CHURCH OF ENGLAND HAS SAID ABOUT SEX AND MARRIAGE

It is a caricature that the Church of England thinks about sex at the expense of everything else, but it is true that human sexuality has taken up a lot of the church's energy in the past thirty years. It is also true that the internal debates about the role of women and of LGBTQIA+ people have often made the church look outdated, prejudiced and oppressive to those outside it. This creates a significant problem for a church which wants to share a gospel of love and salvation with its neighbours.

It could be argued that, from the postwar period until the mid-1980s, Anglican leadership was more liberal and progressive than it appears today. For example, the Archbishop of Canterbury, Michael Ramsey, supported the decriminalisation of sexual acts between men in private following the Wolfenden Report to parliament in the 1950s.

In this issue, as with others such as contraception, abortion and divorce, the Established Church, with a role in the lawmaking of parliament, has tried to steer a course between an individual's right to freedom of conscience and the wider good of society. Similarly, a distinction has been made between what is considered a crime and what the church teaches as morally wrong.

The Church of England does not have a formal body for deciding doctrine, unlike the Roman Catholic Congregation for the Doctrine of the Faith. Instead, matters of doctrine are enshrined in the teaching of the House of Bishops and in canon law (including the provision of liturgy, that is, religious services) which is debated and agreed by the General Synod. More widely, bishops from across the Anglican family of churches meet together every ten years in a 'Lambeth Conference' at which matters of doctrine and practice are also discussed and statements can be made.

There have been four reports to the church on marriage, in 1971, 1978, 1988 and 2000; most were reactions to changes in the law about divorce, although the 1988 report[1] was also concerned with cohabitation. None of these reports attempted a reformulation of the theology of marriage, although all to a greater or lesser extent made pastoral provision for those whose situations fell outside the strictures of traditional teaching. In other words, although marriage is still understood to be the lifelong union of one man with one woman, it has become increasingly simple to be married in church following divorce, and sanctions on those who cohabit prior to marriage have almost completely disappeared.

Since the decriminalisation of homosexual acts in 1967, there have been four reports on homosexuality, in 1970, 1979, 1989 and 2013. The mind of the church has been expressed formally on two occasions, first, in a motion passed at General Synod in November 1987 which affirmed the 'biblical and traditional teaching on chastity and fidelity in personal relationships' in which the only proper expression of sexual activity is in permanent and faithful marriage.[2] Everything which falls short of this ideal, including sex outside marriage, divorce and homosexual activity, should be met by a call for repentance. In 1991, the House of Bishops produced a statement, *Issues in Human Sexuality*,[3] which reinforced the traditional teaching. While it was, arguably, more sympathetic to the status of LGBTQIA+ people, the report concluded that 'Heterosexuality and homosexuality are not equally congruous with the observed order of creation or with the insights of revelation as the church engages with these in the light of her pastoral ministry.'[4] The Lambeth Conference, meeting in 1998, reaffirmed this position, but encouraged a listening process for Christians of different views to engage with one another and, importantly, to listen to the views and experiences of LGBTQIA+ people.

While the church remained, at least in its formal pronouncements, fixed in its views, as we have seen, civil society was changing rapidly. As an institutional church, the Church of England was forced to respond.

So it was that when the government created civil partnerships, with a parallel legal status to civil marriage, in 2005, the church had to make a decision about the status of such relationships. While refusing to offer a religious service to mark such partnerships, the church took a more pastorally accommodating view of them, particularly for ordinary lay people. So, the House of Bishops made it clear that, while the same standards apply to all, the church did not want to exclude from its fellowship those lay people of gay or lesbian orientation who, in conscience, were unable to accept that a life of sexual abstinence was required of them and instead chose to enter into a faithful, committed relationship. 'The House considers that lay people who have registered civil partnerships ought not to be asked to give assurances about the nature of their relationship before being admitted to baptism, confirmation and communion.'[5]

The House of Bishops were able to do this, and indeed to allow clergy to enter civil partnerships, because they could claim that such partnerships were different in quality and status from marriage. A civil partnership, unlike a marriage, cannot be annulled on the basis of non-consummation. If not having sex is not a reason for dissolving a civil partnership, it follows logically that they can be celibate relationships.

When the government introduced the Marriage (Same Sex Couples) Act in 2013, this created a different challenge, since it changed the definition of marriage, and as we have seen, this is something that the church has resisted consistently for the last fifty years. The introduction of equal marriage created a huge gulf between what the state sanctions and the church's stated beliefs. This leaves a challenge for the church and for its individual members in acting with a good conscience, not only in their own lives but as they view the behaviour of others around them.

Currently, the church has once again entered a period of study and discernment with a number of working parties meeting to consider the theological, social and scientific aspects of human sexuality before any further changes in liturgy or practice will be sanctioned either by the House of Bishops or the General Synod.

NOTES

INTRODUCTION
1   www.sharedconversations.org

CHAPTER 1
1   www.theguardian.com/commentisfree/2016/mar/23/gender-fluid-generation-young-people-male-female-trans
2   www.ons.gov.uk/peoplepopulationandcommunity/culturalidentity/sexuality/bulletins/sexualidentityuk/2015

CHAPTER 2
1   www.ipsos.com/sites/default/files/ct/news/documents/2017-11/trust-in-professions-veracity-index-2017-slides.pdf
2   Rasmus Kleis Nielsen, 'Where do people get their news?', https://medium.com/oxford-university/where-do-people-get-their-news-8e85oaodea03
3   www.ipsos.com/sites/default/files/ct/news/documents/2017-11/trust-in-professions-veracity-index-2017-slides.pdf
4   The Virginia Report to the 1988 Lambeth Conference, cited in Philip Groves, ed., The Anglican Communion and Homosexuality (London: SPCK, 2008), p.83.
5   The Roman Catholic Church did not admit that it was wrong to sanction Galileo until 1992, over 350 years after he was excommunicated.
6   'If you are a preacher of mercy, do not preach an imaginary but the true mercy. If the mercy is true, you must therefore bear the true, not an imaginary sin. God does not save those who are only imaginary sinners. Be a sinner, and let your sins be strong (sin boldly), but let your trust in Christ be stronger, and rejoice in Christ who is the victor over sin, death, and the world.' Luther, letter to Philip Melanchthon, http://www.projectwittenberg.org/pub/resources/text/wittenberg/luther/letsinsbe.txt

CHAPTER 3
1   *Catechism of the Catholic Church*, paragraph 2333.
2   House of Bishops, *Some Issues in Human Sexuality: A Guide to the Debate* (London: Church House Publishing, 1991), www.chpublishing.co.uk/uploads/documents/0715138685.pdf

3   Walter Bruggemann, *Genesis: Interpretation: A Bible Commentary for Teaching and Preaching* (Atlanta, GA: John Knox Press, 1982).

4   Phyllis Trible, *God and the Rhetoric of Sexuality* (Philadelphia, PA: Fortress Press, 1978); *Texts of Terror* (London: SCM Press, 2002).

5   www.law.csuohio.edu/sites/default/files/shared/eve_and_adam-text_analysis-2.pdf

6   Phyllis Trible, *God and the Rhetoric of Sexuality* (Philadelphia, PA: Fortress Press, 1978).

7   Tina Beattie, *God's Mother, Eve's Advocate* (London: Continuum, 2002).

8   This position is very clearly argued by Vaughn Roberts in his book *Transgender* (Epsom: The Good Book Company, 2016).

9   Ian Paul, 'Will we be male and female in the new creation?' www.psephizo.com/biblical-studies/will-we-be-male-and-female-in-the-new-creation

10 Adrian Thatcher, *God, Sex and Gender* (London: Wiley-Blackwell, 2011).

11 Graham Ward, 'Bodies: The Displaced Body of Jesus Christ,' pp. 163–1181, in J. Milbank, C. Pickstock and G. Ward, eds, *Radical Orthodoxy* (London: Routledge, 1999).

12 Rachel describes her experience in her autobiography *Dazzling Darkness: Gender, Sexuality, Illness and God* (Glasgow: Wild Goose Publications, 2012) (for this particular quote, see p. 41). Other transgender Christians tell their story in Christina Beardsley and Michelle O'Brien, eds, *This Is My Body: Hearing the Theology of Transgender Christians* (London: Darton Longman and Todd, 2016).

13 Free & Equal: United Nations for LGBT Equality, *Fact Sheet: Intersex*, https://unfe.org/system/unfe-65-Intersex_Factsheet_ENGLISH.pdf

14 *Report to Fusion.Net: January 2015 Survey of Millennials*, https://fusiondotnet.files.wordpress.com/2015/02/fusion-poll-gender-spectrum.pdf

CHAPTER 4

1   Augustine, who had a long relationship and fathered a son with his mistress but never married her, looked back on his life after his conversion and confessed that he had often pleaded with God, 'Grant me chastity and self control, but please not yet.' *The Confessions of St Augustine* (translated by Maria Boulding; London: Hodder and Stoughton, 1977), Book VIII, paragraph 17, p. 198).

2   This is a recurring theme in *The Interior Castle* by Teresa of Avila (translated by E. Allison Peers; New York: Dover Publications, [1577] 2007).

3   The scientist Andrew Newburg has found evidence of increased dopamine levels among religious people at prayer, but others have suggested that the value of meditation (in particular) is in reducing dopamine levels which have become overstimulated in our modern world. www.andrewnewberg.com/research-blog/2013/9/26/how-does-meditation-change-our-brains

4   Renee Descartes, in the 17th century, sought to show that because we can think about our existence, even if the thought is questioning reality, we must exist. This idea is summed up in the phrase *cogito, ergo sum*, or 'I think, therefore I am.' Immanuel Kant, in the following century, built on the idea that humans should base their ideas about the world on their

experience, and deduce general truths from the particular. Immanuel Kant, *The Moral Law* (translated by H.J. Paton; Oxford: Routledge Modern Classics, [1785] 2005).

5   www.who.int/reproductivehealth/publications/general/lancet_2.pdf

6   Helen Fisher, *Why We Love* (Richmond, BC: Holt Paperbacks, 2005) and see also her TED talks, www.ted.com/talks/helen_fisher_studies_the_brain_in_love and www.ted.com/talks/helen_fisher_tells_us_why_we_love_cheat

7   Immanuel Kant, *The Moral Law* (translated by H.J. Paton; Oxford: Routledge Modern Classics, [1785] 2005), p. 42.

8   Ibid., p.209.

9   www.natsal.ac.uk/natsal-3.aspx

10   Steve Peters, *The Chimp Paradox* (London: Penguin, 2013), and see also Daniel Kahneman, *Thinking Fast and Slow* (London: Penguin, 2012).

CHAPTER 5

1   Congregation for the Doctrine of the Faith, *Persona Humana*, 1975. www.vatican.va/roman_curia/congregations/cfaith/documents/rc_con_cfaith_doc_19751229_persona-humana_en.html

2   Jeffrey John, *Permanent, Faithful, Stable: Christian Same-Sex Partnerships* (London: Darton Longman and Todd, 2003).

3   The Archbishops' Council, *Grace and Disagreement: Shared Conversations in Human Sexuality: A Reader* (London: the Archbishops' Council, 2015), pp. 24–51.

4   Congregation for the Doctrine of the Faith, *On the Pastoral Care of Homosexual Persons*, letter to Roman Catholic bishops, 1986.

5   Alfred Kinsey, Wardell B. Pomeroy and Clyde E. Martin, *Sexual Behaviour in the Human Male* (Bloomington, IN: Indiana University Press, [1948] 1998).

6   Office for National Statistics, 'Sexual Identity, UK: 2016', www.ons.gov.uk/peoplepopulationandcommunity/culturalidentity/sexuality/bulletins/sexualidentityuk/2016

7   https://newrepublic.com/article/61118/the-end-gay-culture

8   Ann P. Haas, Mickey Eliason, Vickie M. Mays, Robin M. Mathy *et al.*, 'Suicide and suicide risk in lesbian, gay, bisexual, and transgender populations: Review and recommendations,' *Journal of Homosexuality*, www.ncbi.nlm.nih.gov/pmc/articles/PMC3662085

CHAPTER 6

1   Daniel Block, 'The Patricentric Vision of Family Order,' in Thomas A. Noble, Sarah K. Whittle and Philip S. Johnston, eds, *Marriage, Family and Relationships* (London: Apollos, 2017).

2   Commonly known as the *Westminster Directory*.

3   Office for National Statistics, 'Sexual Identity, UK: 2016', www.ons.gov.uk/peoplepopulationandcommunity/culturalidentity/sexuality/bulletins/sexualidentityuk/2016

4   www.yourchurchwedding.org/article/your-children-are-welcome
5   Rowan Williams, *The Body's Grace*, 1989, www.anglican.ca/wp-content/uploads/2010/10/the-bodys-grace.pdf

CHAPTER 7

1   www.bridesmagazine.co.uk/planning/general/planning-service/2013/01/average-cost-of-wedding
2   Rowan Williams, *Being Human* (London: SPCK, 2018).
3   https://i.redd.it/osof96hutqlo1.jpg, widely reproduced on social media, accessed 28 April 2018.
4   James Alison, *Raising Abel* (London: SPCK, 2010).
5   C.S. Lewis, *Miracles*, cited by Ian Paul in 'Will we be male and female in the new creation?' www.psephizo.com/biblical-studies/will-we-be-male-and-female-in-the-new-creation

APPENDIX

1   *An Honourable Estate: The Doctrine of Marriage According to English Law* (The Hoare Report), Central Board of Finance of the Church of England GS 801 (London: Church House Publishing, 1988).
2   *1987 General Synod Motion* (The Higton Motion), archive.churchsociety.org/issues_new/documents/Text_1987Sexuality.pdf
3   House of Bishops, *Issues in Human Sexuality: A Statement by the House of Bishops* (London: Church House Publishing, 1991).
4   Cited in: House of Bishops, *Some Issues in Human Sexuality: A Guide to the Debate* (London: Church House Publishing, 2003), www.chpublishing.co.uk/uploads/documents/0715138685.pdf
5   *Civil Partnerships: A Pastoral Statement from the House of Bishops of the Church of England*, 2005, https://www.churchofengland.org/sites/default/files/2017-11/House%20of%20Bishops%20Statement%20on%20Civil%20Partnerships%202005.pdf

FURTHER READING

Books

The Archbishops' Council. *Grace and Disagreement: Shared Conversations in Human Sexuality: A Reader* (London: the Archbishops' Council, 2015)

Beardsley, Christina and O'Brien, Michelle, eds. *This Is My Body: Hearing the Theology of Transgender Christians* (London: Darton Longman and Todd, 2016)

Bruggemann, Walter. *Genesis: Interpretation: A Bible Commentary for Teaching and Preaching* (Atlanta, GA: John Knox Press, 1982)

Cornwall, Susannah. *Sexuality: The Inclusive Church Resource* (London: Darton Longman and Todd, 2014)

Davison, Andrew. *Amazing Love: Theology for Understanding Discipleship, Sexuality and Mission* (London: Darton Longman and Todd, 2016)

Fisher, Helen. *Why We Love* (Richmond, BC: Holt Paperbacks, 2005)

Groves, Philip, ed. *The Anglican Communion and Homosexuality* (London: SPCK, 2008)

John, Jeffrey. *Permanent, Faithful, Stable: Christian Same-Sex Partnerships* (London: Darton Longman and Todd, 2003)

Lain-Priestly, Rosemary. *Gender: The Inclusive Church Resource* (London: Darton, Longman and Todd, 2015)

Mann, Rachel. *Dazzling Darkness: Gender, Sexuality, Illness and God* (Glasgow: Wild Goose Publications, 2012)

Marsh, Michael. *On Being Human: Distinctiveness, Dignity, Disability and Disposal* (Alresford: Iff Books, 2015)

Moore, Gareth. *A Question of Truth: Christianity and Homosexuality* (London: Continuum, 2003)

Roberts, Vaughn. *Transgender* (Epsom: The Good Book Company, 2016)

Thatcher, Adrian. *God, Sex and Gender: An Introduction* (London: Wiley-Blackwell, 2011)

Trible, Phyllis. *God and the Rhetoric of Sexuality* (Philadelphia, PA: Fortress Press, 1978)

Vernon, Mark. *The Meaning of Friendship* (London: Palgrave Macmillan, 2010)

Williams, Rowan. *Being Human: Bodies, Minds, Persons* (London: SPCK, 2018)

Wilson, Alan. *More Perfect Union: Understanding Same-Sex Marriage* (London: Darton Longman and Todd, 2014)

Church of England reports

An Honourable Estate: The Doctrine of Marriage According to English Law (The Hoare Report). Central Board of Finance of the Church of England GS 801 (London: Church House Publishing, 1988)

The House of Bishops, Some Issues in Human Sexuality: A Guide to the Debate. Discussion document from the House of Bishops' Group on *Issues in Human Sexuality* (London: Church House Publishing, 2003)

Online articles

Bailey, J. Michael, Vasey, Paul L., Diamond, Lisa M., Breedlove, S. Marc, Vilain, Eric and Epprecht, Marc. *Sexual Orientation, Controversy, and Science*. http://journals.sagepub.com/doi/pdf/10.1177/1529100616637616

Martin, Dale. 'Marriage, Family, Sex, and Women in Paul's Letters' [Video file]. Chapter 1 in 'RLST 152: Introduction to the New Testament History and Literature', Lecture 19. https://oyc.yale.edu/religious-studies/rlst-152/lecture-19

National Geographic, 'How Science is Helping Us Understand Gender.' www.nationalgeographic.com/magazine/2017/01/how-science-helps-us-understand-gender-identity

Task Force on the Study of Marriage, Report to the 78th General Convention of the Episcopal Church, Essay 3: A History of Christian Marriage. http://s3.amazonaws.com/dfc_attachments/public/documents/3223195/Marriage_Report_Essay_3.pdf

Williams, Rowan. *The Body's Grace*. www.anglican.ca/wp-content/uploads/2010/10/the-bodys-grace.pdf